The Gold Standard

The Gold Standard

An Austrian Perspective

Edited by
Llewellyn H. Rockwell, Jr.
The Ludwig von Mises Institute
Auburn University

Introduction by
Leland B. Yeager
Auburn University

Lexington Books
D.C. Heath and Company/Lexington, Massachusetts/Toronto

Library of Congress Cataloging in Publication Data

Main entry under title:

The Gold standard.

Includes index.
Contents: The case for a genuine gold dollar/by Murray N. Rothbard—The monetary writings of Carl Menger/by Hans F. Sennholz—Ludwig von Mises and the gold standard/by Richard Ebeling—[etc.]
  1. Gold standard—Addresses, essays, lectures. I. Rockwell, Llewellyn H.
HG297.G626 1985   332.4'222   84-48567
ISBN 0-669-09693-8 (alk. paper)

Published simultaneously in Canada
Printed in the United States of America on acid-free paper
International Standard Book Number: 0-669-09693-8
Library of Congress Catalog Card Number: 84-48567

Contents

Preface

In November 1983, more than four hundred scholars, students, policy-makers, journalists, and members of the public gathered in the Caucus Room of the Cannon House Office Building on Capitol Hill to participate in the first academic conference of its kind: *The Gold Standard: An Austrian Perspective*, sponsored by the Ludwig von Mises Institute.

Since that time, there has been increasing interest in nonmainstream views of the present monetary system and possible alternatives. This book—which incorporates the papers delivered at the conference—is only one example.

I wish to thank the distinguished patrons of the Mises Institute who made the conference and therefore this book possible: Mr. Henry N. Anderson; Arnold Bernhard & Company, Inc.; Dr. and Mrs. Orville J. Davis; Mr. Edward Durell; Dunn's Commodities, Inc.; Mr. Winthrop French; Mr. Sheldon Rose; and two anonymous contributors.

Ambassador J. William Middendorf II and Congressman Philip M. Crane also gave indispensable help, as did Ms. Donna Dudek of Dudek Communications, Inc.; Ms. Debra Stover and Mr. Paul Culler of Congressman Ron Paul's office; and Ms. Pat Heckman and Ms. Mardi Orr of the Mises Institute.

Thanks are also due to the conference participants not included in this volume: Professor Richard H. Timberlake, the University of Georgia; Mr. Maxwell Newton, the *New York Post*; Professor Stephen O. Morrell, Auburn University; Governor J. Charles Partee, the Federal Reserve System; Professor Don Bellante, Auburn University; Mr. George Selgin, New York University; Mr. Michael Montgomery, Auburn University; Ms. Pamela Brown, Auburn University; Dr. Augustin Navarro, Mexico City; Mrs. Carol Paul, Lake Jackson, Texas; Mr. Burton S. Blumert, Center for Libertarian Studies; Mrs. Ludwig von Mises, New York City; Professor Robert F. Hebert, Auburn University; Professor Leonard Liggio, Institute for Humane Studies; and Mr. Donald Boudreaux, Auburn University.

I also wish to thank Dr. Bruce Katz, Ms. Martha Cleary, and Ms. Susan Cummings of Lexington Books, and Ms. Cynthia M. Dunlevy of The Mises Institute, for all their help, hard work, and patience.

Not too many years ago, the academic world recognized only two sides to the monetary argument: discretion or monetarism. But now the gold standard must be considered as well, and the Austrian scholars whose papers comprise this book have helped make this true.

Introduction

Leland B. Yeager

This book grew out of a conference sponsored by the Ludwig von Mises Institute of Auburn University and held on Capitol Hill in Washington in November 1983.

In their chapters Ron Paul, Murray Rothbard, and Lawrence White offer their own views on a desirable form of gold standard and how to attain it. Hans Sennholz and Joseph Salerno bring two other economists into this discussion—Carl Menger and Michael Heilperin, respectively—much as if they too had been taking part in the conference. In their expositions and critiques of Menger's and Heilperin's views, Sennholz and Salerno of course develop ideas of their own. Richard Ebeling reviews several "Austrian" themes, as well as the suggestions of Ludwig von Mises for the complete removal of state control, influence, and power over money and banking. In Mises' view, monetary reform could not stand alone. As he said, in Ebeling's paraphrase, "A free money could only prevail, ultimately, in a free society."

While also favoring—or expecting monetary freedom to bring—some sort of gold standard, Roger Garrison confronts an issue not discussed by the other authors. For this reason, I will comment on his chapter first and then use its main point for a transition to the overlapping themes of the other chapters.

Garrison reviews some published estimates of the resource costs of a gold standard. In the spirit of the methods employed, let us note that base money has amounted to between 5 and 6 percent of annual gross national product in the United States in recent years and suppose that gold becomes the sole base money. (That supposition probably overstates the future role of gold, for it assumes that paper money becomes fully replaced or fully backed by gold.) Suppose further that keeping the price level stable requires money, and so the monetary gold stock, to grow in step with real GNP at full employment, say at 3 percent a year. Six percent times 3 percent is less than one-fifth of 1 percent. Resources worth that much of GNP would have to go each year to producing gold (or earning it from abroad). At the other extreme, however, the monetary gold stock might remain constant, with no gold being produced at home, acquired from abroad, or diverted from nonmonetary uses. All additions to the *real* money stock would then come through a declining price level, and no resources would go for acquiring additional monetary gold. The costs mentioned so far thus lie between zero and a small fraction of 1 percent of real income.

These may not be the only costs. The real stocks of money and particularly of monetary gold must continue being held, year after year. Some of the population's propensity to save or hold wealth is thus diverted away from creating and using productive capital goods. So some economists have theorized, anyway, including Maurice Allais and James Tobin. We may be uncertain whether this argument is valid; but, purely for illustration, let us estimate the cost it indicates by applying an interest rate, say 10 percent, to the assumed 6 percent of the value of GNP tied up in holding monetary gold.

The resulting 0.6 percent, even combined with the more understandable cost previously estimated, amounts to under 1 percent of GNP. Trying out other plausible parameters would still yield an estimate of the same order of magnitude. Intuition does not tell me whether such a number is large or small.

Garrison properly observes that the costs of producing and holding gold are not confined to a gold standard. People hold gold as a hedge against inflation under systems of paper money. Garrison might well have mentioned, also, the resources devoted to dubious collectibles, to investment publications and conferences, and to other efforts to cope with the uncertainties of an inflationary environment. "Ragged inflation" (as Axel Leijonhufvud calls it) under government fiat money imposes still other costs and inefficiencies.

For this and other reasons, I share Garrison's lack of fascination with cost estimates of the sort illustrated in his chapter and again here. Precise numbers are hardly decisive for policy choice. If the gold standard would provide all the advantages claimed for it, including protection against government ruination of money, while no alternative system performed as well, the resource costs would be worth paying.

Garrison properly brings broader categories of benefits and costs into the discussion. The costs of any system include its opportunity costs, that is, the benefits of alternative systems forgone by adopting it instead.

This observation invites comparison of alternative systems. This book's authors not only contrast the gold standard with fiat money but also describe different versions of the gold standard. Several authors warn against pseudo gold standards, such as the "gold price rule" proposed by some supply-siders, which would apparently have the Federal Reserve aim its open-market operations at stabilizing the price of gold.

Ron Paul argues that circulating gold coins are essential to a genuine gold standard. A dollar defined in gold is not enough; it is subject to being redefined. "The key to the government's power to manipulate money is its control over the definition of the word 'dollar.'" Dr. Paul would like to see privately minted gold coins (along with government coins) denominated in units of weight. The separation of their denominations from the dollar denominations of government currency would be instructive. If only the government would get out of the way, a new gold standard could arise from the free market itself.

Paul recommends denominations of one troy ounce and fractions of it, like full and fractional Krugerrands. To me, the esthetics of gold coinage appeals more than the economics; but I do find the rigamarole of troy and avoirdupois ounces, of 480 and 437.5 grains, confusing and messy. Metric units are neater. (The preferences of the public should ultimately decide the units, of course, but this member of the public is entitled to express his preferences and try to influence those of his fellows.)

If we are to have a gold standard, the monetary unit should be the gram (or possibly milligram) of gold. It would be more difficult and embarrassing for the government to decree a cut in gold content of the gram than of the dollar. Gold coins might appear in denominations of 50, 20, 10, 5, and 2 grams. The largest would be 1-2/3 times the size of the old $20 gold piece, the smallest 1-1/3 times the size of the gold dollar minted from 1849 to 1889 (which was an inconveniently small coin). At a gold price of $300 per troy ounce, the 50-gram and 2-gram pieces would be worth $482.27 and $19.29 respectively. As Paul notes, such high-valued coins would be unlikely to circulate very actively; but they could serve in financial transactions and as a medium for redeeming banknotes and bank deposits.

Hans Sennholz reminds us of Carl Menger's theory of the origin of money, of Menger's view that money serves primarily as medium of exchange, its other functions being derivative, and of his advocacy of Austria-Hungary's shift, in 1892, from fiat money to a (quasi) gold standard. Menger, like other members of the Establishment of his time, considered gold the most modern monetary standard and the one most appropriate for advanced countries; silver and paper were for backward countries.

Menger did not insist on 100 percent gold money or anything close. For Austria-Hungary as for other European countries, he was content with "gold-plated" money. It consisted, figuratively speaking, of a paper core covered by a layer of subsidiary coins, in turn covered by a thin layer of silver coins, and finally covered by an outer layer of gold. Sennholz might have added that Menger had few complaints about the serviceability of Austria's paper gulden for domestic business. Concern over exchange-rate fluctuations, together with considerations of national prestige, made him favor moving onto gold.

Murray Rothbard wants to separate money and banking from the state. Although recognizing how nonweight names of money units facilitate government manipulation of money, Rothbard nevertheless doubts that privately minted gold coins denominated in grams or ounces would catch on. Americans are accustomed to "dollars" and will cling to them. The dollar must be redefined as a definite quantity of gold and its definition then fixed eternally.

To move gold from government vaults into the hands of the public, Rothbard wants the gold content of the dollar set so low that all Federal Reserve notes and deposits could be redeemed in full. Requiring banks to hold 100 percent reserves against their notes and checkable deposits, which Rothbard seems to want, would entail a still higher dollar price of gold (around $1,700 an ounce, Rothbard calculates).

So high a value would preclude routine circulation of gold coins, but the resource costs of gold reserves might be significant after all. (Rothbard presumably does not want severe depreciation of the purchasing power of the dollar in the process of transition.) The transition would presumably have to be coordinated carefully with foreign countries to avoid massive gold shipments to the United States or great disruptions of exchange rates.

Michael Heilperin, as reported by Joseph Salerno, went beyond David Hume's theory of shifts in national price levels and achieved a good if not entirely satisfactory insight into the role of the real-balance or direct-spending effect in the process of automatic balance-of-payments adjustment under a gold standard. Heilperin also saw the perversity of diluting gold's monetary discipline under a gold exchange standard as practiced in line with the Genoa resolutions of 1922 and the Bretton Woods agreement of 1944. He predicted that the Bretton Woods system would promote worldwide inflation and chronic balance-of-payments disequilibria. (In Salerno's felicitous language, the system did go through "a slow-motion crash" from 1960 to 1971.) Heilperin foresaw the disappointing performance of the floating exchange rates that have prevailed since 1973.

Salerno himself is wary of a mere pseudo gold standard. Yet Heilperin, curiously, seems not to have been, or not consistently. He offered a qualified defense of the Bretton Woods system against the criticisms of traditional gold-standard advocates like Melchior Palyi; he considered it a first small step toward the international cooperation necessary for a world gold standard. Salerno calls Heilperin a "monetary constructivist."

Lacking Carl Menger's insights into the origin of money, he regarded money as a deliberate construction of the politico-legal system. He viewed the historical gold standard as the product of a government price-fixing scheme. Rather than full convertibility of money into gold coins, he favored a Ricardian gold bullion standard. Instead of wanting a monetary unit defined as an immutable quantity of gold, he accepted changing the "price" of gold as a policy tool for dealing with severe balance-of-payments difficulties. Heilperin thought that the principal monetary function of gold was to meet deficits in international payments. Limiting the potential for monetary inflation was a subsidiary purpose, and he saw no purpose for a gold standard in a closed economy.

Historical evolution, says Lawrence White, speaks for gold or silver as money. Furthermore, a gold standard is inadequate without free banking—free competition in the issue of redeemable banknotes and deposits. A plurality of issuers minimizes the chances for money-supply errors. (Ludwig von Mises saw the same point, as Ebeling reminds us.) Interbank settlement of amounts due on notes and checks routinely presented at the clearinghouse gives each bank both information and incentive to correct promptly any deviation of its money issue from the quantity that the public is willing to hold.

This feedback process is absent when a central bank monopolizes the issue of banknotes and when its own liabilities constitute the reserves of the commercial banks. An overexpansion of notes and deposits of the central bank will not find its way into the clearing mechanism and thereby rapidly manifest itself. Instead, it will support multiple expansion of money and credit by the commercial banks. Only gradually will a balance-of-payments deficit and an external drain of gold signal the central bank to reverse its course. The belated reversal is likely to depress output and employment.

Under free banking, White recognizes, banks will hold merely fractional reserves of gold against their notes and deposits. He challenges Murray Rothbard's belief that sound jurisprudence and ethics practically demand 100 percent reserves. Someone committed to the ethic of individual sovereignty is hardly consistent in wanting to bar banks and their customers from making whatever contractual arrangements they can agree on.

White's case for free banking, as presented here and in his *Free Banking in Britain* (cited in his note 11), is persuasive to me. Less persuasive, and more challenging, is his condemnation of any government influence favoring a monetary unit defined otherwise than as a quantity of gold or silver. Such an influence would exemplify what White calls the "macroinstrumental" approach to judging monetary systems. A macroinstrumentalist views monetary institutions as tools to be designed or redesigned by govenment policymakers. He judges among alternatives solely by comparing how desirable the various statistical time series are that he expects them to generate.

White favors the "microsovereignty" approach instead. That approach asks how well a particular system serves the interests, seen by themselves, of the individuals who use money. A monetary system is a set of institutions for supplying the particular good called money. Why, White asks, should money be treated differently from any other good—say, playing cards? "No proper economist, speaking as an economist, would presume to judge the goodness of the current American playing card ... system by contrasting its characteristics to a list of characteristics he thought desirable."

But money has more of a collective aspect than playing cards. The individual's choice in money depends largely on what sort others are already using. (Menger's theory of the evolution of money actually illuminates this point, as White even recognizes in saying that "each trader finds it most convenient to use as a medium of exchange the item or items most readily accepted by other traders.") The individual's choice is not necessarily the sort of money he would think best if others would go along with him, not necessarily what he and others would prefer if they could decide all together.

Analogies are available. People might leave themselves more daylight hours after work on summer evenings by individually scheduling all their activities one hour earlier. Such decentralized revision of interlocking schedules would probably prove too difficult, but that fact does not imply disapproval of Daylight Saving Time, collectively adopted. People might wish, for their own sake or their children's, that they and their fellow citizens spoke some other language (a simpler or a more internationally prevalent one); yet each individual will be reluctant to go first in switching away from the local language. Most individuals might separately prefer that parties were less alcoholic, yet each will continue attending and giving parties of the kind favored by inertia. When goods or activities with a collective aspect are in question, then, individual choice does not necessarily indicate individual preference. If these other examples seem strained, the reason probably is that money itself provides the best example.

Continued use of the national currency even in extreme inflations illustrates the inertia that favors whatever money currently exists. Rothbard recognizes it when he envisages retaining the dollar, with a new gold definition, instead of replacing it as monetary unit by a weight of gold. Yet some economists of the Austrian school (like Gerald O'Driscoll, writing in the *Cato Journal*, Spring 1983) cite failure of indexing to be widely adopted as evidence that Americans do not particularly desire a stable unit of account. Such a line of argument, ignoring the "Who goes first?" problem that entrenches existing practices, would count against the gold standard itself: If it is so desirable, why haven't private contracts already reinstated it?

Another distinctive aspect of money is that imbalance between its supply and demand has more far-reaching consequences than imbalance on the market for playing cards or any other ordinary good. Money lacks a specific price of its own and market of its own on which supply and demand can come to a focus and straightforwardly correct any imbalance. Because money is the medium of exchange, routinely traded on all ordinary markets, imbalance between its supply and demand shows up on those markets, adversely affecting quantities of goods traded and so quantities produced. A disequilibrium value of the money unit has to be corrected through a painful roundabout process of fragmented and delayed adjustments in myriads of separate but interdependent prices.

This absurdity characterizes both a fiat money unit and also, though possibly in lesser degree, a unit defined as a quantity of gold. Theory and abundant historical evidence point to remediable defects in the monetary system as the chief source of macroeconomic disorders, including inflation, depression, and heavy unemployment.

The ordinary person, untutored in economics, is hardly in a position to have grasped these points already, to decide what sort of money would be best for him and his fellows by affording the best macroeconomic performance, and then to make his decision count through his individual behavior on the market. Why blind oneself to this obvious truth by individualist rhetoric? Despite White's analogy about playing cards, it simply is *not* presumptuous of an economist to examine the performance characteristics of alternative systems and try to enlighten the preferences of his fellow citizens. Engaging in scholarly and popular discussion is not at all the same thing as wanting to play dictator.

Regrettably, perhaps, the government is a major force in defining and using weights and measures and particularly in using and shaping the monetary system. If governments, with their piecemeal and haphazard interventions over the centuries, had not imposed their present-day dominance, we probably would have enjoyed a largely spontaneous and a healthier monetary evolution.

But we are where we are now. Any reform must start here. The manner in which the government disengages from its current domination of money is bound to influence even the free evolution of what comes next. Since the government must unavoidably exert some such nudge or other, good sense demands considering what sort of nudge is desirable and what sort undesirable. It is a cop-out to say "Let the market decide."

The "market's" decision is bound to be affected by just how the government disengages. As Rothbard suggests in an only slightly different context, considered government action to dismantle earlier interventions is not anti-individualist, statist, or "constructivist."

Lawrence White alludes in this volume to a criterion of the desirability of particular monetary institutions that he and other economists of the Austrian school have explicitly urged in other writings: Did those institutions evolve spontaneously in the past, or could they have done so, or could they evolve spontaneously in the future? To insist on such a criterion may express a philosophy or a historical sentiment, but not an economic assessment. Past government interventions, however unwise, have foreclosed the path of completely spontaneous evolution. The particular manner of government disengagement will unavoidably affect the institutions of the future. (Rothbard, in his discussion of the path back to the gold standard, shows that he knows this. Mises knew it too, as Ebeling's discussion reminds us.) It is senseless to disregard the likely performance characteristics of alternative institutions. Why burden the market economy and jeopardize people's productivity, freedom, and happiness with a monetary system likely to perform poorly?

The alternatives to consider are not just the gold standard and government fiat money. Even conceptions of the gold standard differ widely, as illustrated in this volume by Rothbard's 100 percent standard, White's and Mises' fractional-reserve free banking, Paul's parallel private gold coin standard, Menger's "gold-plated" standard, and Heilperin's gold bullion standard employed as an instrument of government policy. The historical gold standard of a few decades up to World War I also deserves consideration, even though it may be one of those institutions that, once destroyed, cannot be restored as they were; the preconditions, perhaps including necessary ideologies or myths, cannot be reconstructed at will.

More cheerful circumstances also count against attempting that reconstruction. Advances in economic theory, communications, and data processing, as well as many actual or potential financial innovations, have widened the range of free-enterprise-oriented monetary systems (and perhaps moneyless payments systems) to choose among.

One desirable characteristic, I should think, is a steady-sized measure of value, a unit in which the general level of prices is roughly stable. One reason for its desirability is that downward or upward pressures on the price level are symptomatic of monetary disequilibria that also cause the macroeconomic disorders already mentioned.

Some economists of the Austrian school, including contributors to this volume, question this desirability, question the measurability of changes in the general price level, and question the analogy between the unit of account and other units of weights and measures. Yet the unit used in expressing prices, incomes, contractual payments, debts, claims, asset values, and accounts does bear a close analogy with units of length and weight. All such units play vital roles in forming and implementing plans and in coordinating the activities of different persons. If we take seriously the burgeoning literature on various severe but subtle damages wrought by inflation, we should appreciate the importance of a stable unit of account.

Analogies are seldom perfect. A stable unit could not be defined with the precision of the meter or kilogram. One can quibble about the particular price index or particular bundle of goods and services to be used in the definition. A real distinction holds, however, between a unit in which prices of goods and services are clearly rising or falling by any plausible criterion and, on the other hand, a unit whose purchasing-power trend is genuinely in doubt, with some prices steady, others rising, and still others falling under pressures specific to their own markets. The latter state of affairs—bona fide doubt about the direction of any average price trend—would count as achievement of a stable unit and would reflect avoidance of any severe monetary disequilibrium. (Rothbard, incidentally, concedes the measurability of price-level changes when he mentions inflation of about 2 percent a year from 1896 to 1914.)

People do regard the money unit, or unit of account, as the unit for measuring values. They so use it every day. They are not interested in the dollar size or the gold-unit size of a particular price, income, debt, or other accounting magnitude except as it indicates value in relation to a much wider set of goods and services. A unit of variable purchasing power subverts people's calculations and degrades the information supposedly conveyed by prices and accounting.

Several authors in this book, as well as Menger, whose views Sennholz summarizes, do recognize after all, if obliquely, that an unstable unit is undesirable. White, for example, decries unpredictability in the purchasing power of money. Well, unpredictability is associated with instability; and the predictions most likely to be made with confidence are warranted predictions of stability.

One might object, as Rothbard and Garrison seem to do, that the value of anything, even of the monetary unit relative to other goods and services in general, should properly be left to market forces. Failure to agree supposedly betrays ignorance of subjectivist elements in the theory of value. The values attributed to particular goods and services, especially intramarginally, are indeed subjective. Yet the interactions of subjectively motivated behaviors on the market do result in phenomena of an objective character, namely, market prices. One can desire a stable objective exchange value of the unit of account without betraying ignorance of subjectivist economic theory.

Rather than a stable price level, Rothbard would prefer—or expect—a gently declining level, partly on the grounds that such is the natural consequence of rising productivity. Well, rising productivity will cheapen some goods relative to others (notably, consumer goods relative to human effort), but it can hardly cheapen goods and services in general relative to goods and services in general. It is eminently reasonable to desire that each particular price express the market value of the good in question relative to goods and services in general and that, accordingly, the pricing unit bear a stable relation to goods and services in general.

The supposed distinction between influences on the price level coming from the goods side and coming from the money side does not bear much weight, in my judgment; for growth over time in the physical quantities of goods and services to be traded on markets does lead people to increase their demands for money holdings relative to the supply, unless supply somehow keeps pace. In short, economic growth entails a money-side and not just a goods-side influence on the price level, unless the actual nominal quantity of money keeps pace with the quantity demanded.

Some economists of the Austrian school fear serious distortions from the "injection" of new money to ward off pressures toward general price deflation. The underlying analysis—that is, the particular theory of a business cycle formerly urged by Mises and Hayek and still urged in this volume by Salerno and Ebeling—strikes me as unpersuasive. Furthermore, some proposed monetary reforms would neatly bypass the supposed problem of injection effects. I wish I had space to describe them.

In conclusion, I appeal for enlisting Austrian insights in the scholarly appraisal of alternative forms of gold standard—and also of other types of free-market monetary or payments systems. It would do no credit to the Austrian school or the memory of Ludwig von Mises if advocacy of the gold standard should degenerate among his admirers into a mere password recited for mutual identification and encouragement. Economists in his tradition have much of substance to contribute, not just slogans. The authors of this book deserve congratulations for exhibiting that potential and for making good progress in applying Austrian analysis to the assessment of alternative monetary reforms.

The Gold Standard

1

The Case for a Genuine Gold Dollar

Murray N. Rothbard

Inflationary Fiat Paper

For nearly a half-century the United States and the rest of the world have experienced an unprecedented continuous and severe inflation. It has dawned on an increasing number of economists that the fact that over the same half-century the world has been on an equally unprecedented fiat paper standard is no mere coincidence. Never have the world's moneys been so long cut off from their metallic roots. During the century of the gold standard from the end of the Napoleonic wars until World War I, on the other hand, prices generally fell year after year, except for such brief wartime interludes as the Civil War.[1] During wartime, the central governments engaged in massive expansion of the money supply to finance the war effort. In peacetime, on the other hand, monetary expansion was small compared to the outpouring of goods and services attendant upon rapid industrial and economic development. Prices, therefore, were normally allowed to fall. The enormous expenditures of World War I forced all the warring governments to go off the gold standard,[2] and unwillingness to return to a genuine gold standard eventually led to a radical shift to fiat paper money during the financial crisis of 1931–33.

It is my contention that there should be no mystery about the unusual chronic inflation plaguing the world since the 1930s. The dollar is the American currency unit (and the pound sterling, the franc, the mark, and the like, are equivalent national currency units), and since 1933, there have been no effective restrictions on the issue of these currencies by the various nation-states. In effect, each nation-state, since 1933, and especially since the end of all gold redemption in 1971, has had the unlimited right and power to create paper currency which will be legal tender in its own geographic area. It is my contention that if any person or organization ever obtains the monopoly right to create money, that person or organization will tend to use this right to the hilt. The reason is simple: Anyone or any group empowered to manufacture money virtually out of thin air will tend to exercise that right, and with considerable enthusiasm. For the power to create money is a heady and profitable privilege indeed.

The essential meaning of a fiat paper standard is that the currency unit—the dollar, pound, franc, mark, or whatever—consists of paper tickets, marked as "dollars," "pound," and so on, and manufactured by the central government of the nation-state.[3] The government (or its central bank) is able to manufacture those tickets *ad libitum* and essentially costlessly. The cost of the paper and the printing is invariably negligible compared to the value of the currency printed. And if, for some reason, such cost is not negligible, the government can always simply increase the denominations of the bills!

It should be clear that the point of the government's having the power to print money is to monopolize that power. It would simply not do to allow every man, woman, and organization the right to print dollars, and so the government invariably guards its monopoly jealously. It should be noted that government is never so zealous in suppressing crime as when that crime consists of direct injury to its own sources of revenue, as in tax evasion and counterfeiting of its currency. If counterfeiting of currency were not illegal, the nation's supply of dollars or francs would rise toward infinity very rapidly, and the purchasing power of the currency unit itself would be effectively destroyed.[4]

In recent years an increasing number of economists have understandably become disillusioned by the inflationary record of fiat currencies. They have therefore concluded that leaving the government and its central bank power to fine tune the money supply, but abjuring them to use that power wisely in accordance with various rules, is simply leaving the fox in charge of the proverbial henhouse. They have come to the conclusion that only radical measures can remedy the problem, in essence the problem of the inherent tendency of government to inflate a money supply that it monopolizes and creates. That remedy is no less than the strict separation of money and its supply from the state.

Hayek's "Denationalization" of Money

The best known proposal to separate money from the state is that of F.A. Hayek and his followers.[5] Hayek's "denationalization of money" would eliminate legal tender laws, and allow every individual and organization to issue its own currency, as paper tickets with its own names and marks attached. The central government would retain its monopoly over the dollar, or franc, but other institutions would be allowed to compete in the money creation business by offering their own brand name currencies. Thus, Hayek would be able to print Hayeks, the present author to issue Rothbards, and so on. Mixed in with Hayek's suggested legal change is an entrepreneurial scheme by which a Hayek-inspired bank would issue "ducats," which would be issued in such a way as to keep prices in terms of ducats constant. Hayek is confident that his ducat would easily out-compete the inflated dollar, pound, mark, or whatever.

Hayek's plan would have merit if the thing—the commodity—we call "money" were similar to all other goods and services. One way, for exam-ple, to get rid of the inefficient, backward, and sometimes despotic U.S. Postal Service is simply to abolish it; but other free market advocates propose the less radical plan of keeping the post office intact but allow-ing any and all organizations to compete with it. These economists are confident that private firms would soon be able to outcompete the post office. In the past decade, economists have become more sympathetic to deregulation and free competition, so that superficially denationalizing or allowing free competition in currencies would seem viable in analogy with postal services or fire-fighting or private schools.

There is a crucial difference, however, between money and all other goods and services. All other goods, whether they be postal service or candy bars or personal computers, are desired for their own sake, for the utility and value that they yield to consumers. Consumers are therefore able to weigh these utilities against one another on their own personal scales of value. Money, however, is desired not for its own sake, but precisely because it *already* functions as money, so that everyone is con-fident that the money commodity will be readily accepted by any and all in exchange. People eagerly accept paper tickets marked "dollars" not for their aesthetic value, but because they are sure that they will be able to sell those tickets for the goods and services they desire. They can only be sure in that way when the particular name, "dollar," is *already* in use as money.

Hayek is surely correct that a free market economy and a devotion to the right of private property requires that everyone be permitted to issue whatever proposed currency names and tickets they wish. Hayek should be free to issue Hayeks or ducats, and I to issue Rothbards or whatever. But issuance and *acceptance* are two very different matters. No one will accept new currency tickets, as they well might new postal organizations or new computers. These names will not be chosen as currencies pre-cisely because they have not been used as money, or for any other pur-pose, before.

Hayek and his followers have failed completely to absorb the lesson of Ludwig von Mises' "regression theorem," one of the most important theorems in monetary economics.[6] Mises showed, as far back as 1912, that since no one will accept any entity as money unless it had been demanded and exchanged earlier, we must therefore logically go back (regress) to the first day when a commodity became used as money, a medium of exchange. Since by definition the commodity could not have been used as money before that first day, it could only be demanded because it had been used as a nonmonetary commodity, and therefore had a preexisting price, even in the era before it began to be used as a medium. In other words, for any commodity to become used as money, it must have originated as a commodity valued for some nonmonetary purpose, so that it had a stable demand and price before it began to be used as a medium of exchange. In short, money cannot be created out of thin air, by social contract, or by issuing paper tickets with new names on them. Money has to originate as a valuable nonmonetary commodity. In practice, precious metals such as gold or silver, metals in stable and high demand per unit weight, have won out over all other commodities as moneys. Hence, Mises' regression theorem demonstrates that money must originate as a useful nonmonetary commodity on the free market.

But one crucial problem with the Hayekian ducat is that no one will take it. New names on tickets cannot hope to compete with dollars or pounds which originated as units of weight of gold or silver and have now been used for centuries on the market as the currency unit, the medium of exchange, and the instrument of monetary calculation and reckoning.[7]

Hayek's plan for the denationalization of money is Utopian in the worst sense: not because it is radical, but because it would not and could not work. Print different names on paper all one wishes, and these new tickets still would not be accepted or function as money; the dollar (or pound or mark) would still reign unchecked. Even the removal of the legal tender privilege would not work, for the new names would not have emerged out of useful commodities on the free market, as the regression theorem demonstrates they must. And since the government's own currency, the dollar and the like, would continue to reign unchallenged as money, money would not have been denationalized at all. Money would still be nationalized and a creature of the state; there would still be no separation of money and the state. In short, even though hopelessly Utopian, the Hayek plan would scarcely be radical enough, since the current inflationary and state-run system would be left intact.

Even the variant on Hayek whereby private citizens or firms issue gold coins denominated in grams or ounces would not work, and this is true even though the dollar and other fiat currencies originated centuries ago as names of units of weight of gold or silver.[8] Americans have been used to using and reckoning in "dollars" for two centuries, and they will cling to the dollar for the foreseeable future. They will simply not shift away from the dollar to the gold ounce or gram as a currency unit. People will cling doggedly to their customary names for currency; even during runaway inflation and virtual destruction of the currency, the German people clung to the "mark" in 1923 and the Chinese to the "yen" in the 1940s. Even drastic revaluations of the runaway currencies which helped end the inflation kept the original "mark" or other currency name.

Hayek brings up historical examples where more than one currency circulated in the same geographic area at the same time, but none of the examples is relevant to his "ducat" plan. Border regions may accept two *governmental* currencies,[9] but each has legal tender power, and each had been in lengthy use within its own nation. Multicurrency circulation, then, is not relevant to the idea of one or more new private paper currencies. In addition, Hayek might have mentioned the fact that in the United States, until the practice was outlawed in 1857, foreign gold and silver coins as well as private gold coins, circulated as money side by side with official coins. The fact that the Spanish silver dollar had long circulated in America along with Austrian and English specie coins, permitted the new United States to change over easily from pound to dollar reckoning. But again, this situation is not relevant, because all these coins were different weights of gold and silver, and none was fiat government money. It was easy, then, for people to refer the various values of the coins back to their gold or silver weights. Gold and silver had of course long circulated as money, and the pound sterling or dollar were simply different weights of one or the other metals. Hayek's plan is a very different one: the issue of private paper tickets marked by new names and in the hope that they are accepted as money.

If people love and will cling to their dollars or francs, then there is only one way to separate money from the state, to truly denationalize a nation's money. And that is to denationalize the *dollar* (or the mark or franc) itself. Only privatization of the dollar can end the government's inflationary dominance of the nation's money supply.

How, then, can the dollar be privatized or denationalized? Obviously not by making counterfeiting legal. There is only one way: to link the dollar once again to a useful market commodity. Only by changing the definition of the dollar from fiat paper tickets issued by the government to a unit of weight of some market commodity, can the function of issuing money be permanently and totally shifted from government to private hands.

The "Commodity Dollar": A Critique

If it is imperative that the dollar be defined once again as a weight of a market commodity, then what commodity (or commodities) should it be defined as, and what should be the particular weight in which it is set?

In reply, I propose that the dollar be defined as a weight of a single commodity, and that that commodity be gold. Many economists, beginning with Irving Fisher at the turn of the twentieth century, and including Benjamin Graham and an earlier F.A. Hayek, have hankered after some form of "commodity dollar," in which the dollar is defined, not as a weight of a single commodity, but in terms of a "market basket" of two or many more commodities.[10] There are many deep-seated flaws in this approach. In the first place, such a market-basket currency has never emerged spontaneously from the workings of the market. It would have to be imposed (to use a derogatory term from Hayek himself) as a "constructivist" scheme from the top, from government to be inflicted upon the market. Second, and as a corollary, the government would be obviously in charge, since a market-basket currency does not, unlike the use of units of weight in exchange, arise from the free market itself. The government could and would, then, alter the ratios of weights, adjust the various fixed terms, and so forth. Third, the hankering for a fixed market basket is an outgrowth of a strong desire for the government to regulate the economy so as to keep the "price level" constant. As we have seen, the natural tendency of the free market is to lower prices over time, in accordance with growing productivity and increased supplies of goods. There is no good reason for the government to interfere. Indeed, if it does so, it can only create a boom-and-bust business cycle by expanding credit to keep prices artificially higher than they would be on the free market.

Furthermore, there are other grave problems with the commodity-basket approach. There is, for one thing, no such unitary entity as "the price level" which would be kept constant. The entire concept of price level is an artificial construction masking the fact that it can only consist of individual prices, each varying continually in relation to each other.

Irving Fisher's intense desire for a constant price level stemmed from his own fallacious philosophic notion that, just as science is based upon measurable standards (such as a yard comprising 36 inches), so money is supposed to be a measure of values and prices. But since there is no single price level, his very idea, far from being scientific, is a hopeless chimera. The only scientific measurement that properly applies is the currency unit as a true measure of *weight* of the money commodity. Furthermore, the only scientific measure is a definition which, once selected, remains eternally the same: "the pound," or "the yard." Juggling definitions of weight within a market basket violates any proper concept of definition or of measure.[11]

A final and vital flaw in a market-basket dollar is that Gresham's law would result in perpetual shortages and surpluses of different commodities within the market basket. Gresham's law states that any money overvalued by the government (in relation to its market value) will drive out of circulation money undervalued by the government. In short, control of exchange rates has consequences like any other price control: A maximum rate below the free market causes a shortage; a minimum rate set above the market will cause a surplus. From the origin of the United States, the currency was in continuing trouble because the United States was on a bimetallic rather than a gold standard, in short a market basket of two commodities, gold and silver. As is well known, the system never worked, because at one time or another, one or the other precious metal was above or below its world market valuations, and hence one or the other coin or bullion was flowing into the country while the other would disappear. In 1873 partisans of the monometallic gold standard, seeing that silver was soon to be overvalued and hence on the point of driving out gold, put the United States on a virtual single gold standard, a system that was ratified officially in 1900.[12]

One argument used by Fisher, James M. Buchanan, and others holds that the U.S. Constitution mandates the government's using its powers to stabilize the price level. This argument rests on Article I, Section 8 of the Constitution, which gives Congress the power "to coin money, regulate the value thereof..." The argument, absurd at best, disingenuous at worst, and certainly anachronistic treats the framers of the Constitution as if they were modern price-stabilizationist economists, as if they meant by "the value thereof" the purchasing power of the money unit, or its inverse, the price level. From this dubious assumption, these writers derive the alleged constitutional duty of the federal government to intervene in monetary matters so as to stabilize the level of prices. But what the framers meant by "value" was simply the weight and the fineness of coins. It is, after all, the responsibility of every firm to regulate the nature of its own product, and to the extent that the federal government mints coins, it must see to it that the weight and fineness of these coins are what the government says they are.

The Case for a Gold Dollar

We conclude, then, that the dollar must be redefined in terms of a single commodity, rather than in terms of an artificial market basket of two or more commodities. Which commodity, then, should be chosen? In the first place, precious metals, gold and silver, have always been preferred to all other commodities as mediums of exchange where they have been available. It is no accident that this has been the invariable success story of precious metals, which can be partly explained by their superior stable nonmonetary demand, their high value per unit weight, durability, divisibility cognizability, and the other virtues described at length in the first chapter of all money and banking textbooks published before the U.S. government abandoned the gold standard in 1933. Which metal should be the standard, then, silver or gold? There is, indeed, a case for silver, but the weight of argument holds with a return to gold. Silver's increasing relative abundance of supply has depreciated its value badly in terms of gold, and it has not been used as a general monetary metal since the nineteenth century. Gold was *the* monetary standard in most countries until 1914, or even until the 1930s. Furthermore, gold was the standard when the U.S. government in 1933 confiscated the gold of all American citizens and abandoned gold redeemability of the dollar, supposedly only for the duration of the depression emergency. Still further, gold and not silver is still considered a monetary metal everywhere, and governments and their central banks have managed to amass an enormous amount of gold not now in use, but which again could be used as a standard for the dollar, pound, or mark.

This brings up an important corollary. The United States, and other governments, have in effect nationalized gold. Even now, when private citizens are allowed to own gold, the great bulk of that metal continues to be sequestered in the vaults of the central banks.[13] If the dollar is redefined in terms of gold, gold as well as the dollar can be jointly denationalized. But if the dollar is *not* defined as a weight of gold, then how can a denationalization of gold ever take place? Selling the gold stock would be unsatisfactory, since this (1) would imply that the government is entitled to the receipts from the sale and (2) would leave the dollar under the absolute fiat control of the government.

It is important to realize what a definition of the dollar in terms of gold would entail. The definition must be *real* and effective rather than nominal. Thus, the U.S. statutes define the dollar as 1/42.22 gold ounce, but this definition is a mere formalistic accounting device. To be real, the definition of the dollar as a unit of weight of gold must imply that the dollar is interchangeable and therefore redeemable by its issuer in that weight, that the dollar is a demand claim for that weight in gold.

Furthermore, once selected, the definition, whatever it is, must be fixed permanently. Once chosen, there is no more excuse for changing definitions than there is for altering the length of a standard yard or the weight of a standard pound.

Before proceeding to investigate what the new definition or weight of the dollar should be, let us consider some objections to the very idea of the government setting a new definition. One criticism holds it to be fundamentally statist and a violation of the free market for the government, rather than the market, to be responsible for fixing a new definition of the dollar in terms of gold. The problem, however, is that we are now tackling the problem in midstream, *after* the government has taken the dollar off gold, virtually nationalized the stock of gold, and issued dollars for decades as arbitrary and fiat money. Since government has monopolized issue of the dollar, and confiscated the public's gold, only government can solve the problem by jointly denationalizing gold and the dollar. Objection to government's redefining and privatizing gold is equivalent to complaining about the government's repealing its own price controls because repeal would constitute a governmental rather than private action. A similar charge could be leveled at government's denationalizing any product or operation. It is not advocating statism to call for the government's repeal of its own interventions.

A corollary criticism, and a favorite of monetarists, asks why gold standard advocates would have the government "fix the (dollar) price of gold" when they are generally opposed to fixing any other prices. Why leave the market free to determine all prices *except* the price of gold?

But this criticism totally misconceives the meaning of the concept of price. A "price" is the quantity exchanged of one commodity on the market in terms of another. Thus, in barter, if a package of six light bulbs is exchanged on the market for one pound of butter, then the price per light bulb is one-sixth of a pound of butter. Or, if there is monetary exchange, the price of each light bulb will be a certain weight of gold, or, these days, numbers of cents or dollars. The important point is that price is the ratio of quantities of *two commodities* being exchanged. But if money is on a gold standard, the dollar and gold will no longer be two independent commodities, whose price should be free to fluctuate on the market. They will be *one* commodity, one a unit of weight of the other. To call for a "free market" in the "price of gold" is as ludicrous as calling for a free market of ounces in terms of pounds, or inches in terms of yards. How many inches equal a yard is not something subject to daily fluctuations on the free or any other market. The answer is fixed eternally by definition, and what a gold standard entails is a fixed, absolute, unchanging definition as in the case of any other measure or unit of weight. The market necessarily exchanges two different commodities rather than one commodity for itself. To call for a free market in the price of gold would, in short, be as absurd as calling for a fluctuating market price for dollars in terms of cents. How many cents constitute a dollar is no more subject to daily fluctuation and uncertainty than inches in terms of yards. On the contrary, a truly free market in money will exist only when the dollar is once again strictly defined and therefore redeemable in terms of weights of gold. After that, gold will be exchangeable, at freely fluctuating prices, for the weights of all other goods and services on the market.

In short, the very description of a gold standard as "fixing the price of gold" is a grave misinterpretation. In a gold standard, the "price of gold" is not unaccountably fixed by government intervention. Rather, the "dollar," for the past half-century a mere paper ticket issued by the government, will become defined once again as a unit of weight of gold.

Defining the Dollar

If, then, the dollar should once again be defined as a unit of weight of gold, what should the new definition be? It is curious that the growing number of economists and writers who call for a return to the gold standard seem to display little or no interest in what precisely the new weight of the dollar should be. The question is admittedly a controversial one, but even more controversial is the very question of having a gold standard at all. Moreover, it should be realized that there is no hope of ever returning to a gold standard unless the proper weight of the dollar is first decided upon.

From the 1940s to the 1960s, the small body of advocates of a return to gold were grouped in two kindred organizations: the Economists' National Committee for Monetary Policy, and the Gold Standard League. Both were guided by Walter E. Spahr, professor of economics at New York University. In this era, and indeed from 1933 until 1971, the United States was on a fiat standard domestically, but on a curious and highly restricted form of gold standard internationally, in which the United States agreed to redeem dollars held by foreign governments and their central banks in gold at the legally defined rate of $35 per ounce. Foreign individuals or private firms could not redeem their dollar balances in gold, and neither individuals nor governments could redeem their dollars in gold coin, since such coin was no longer being issued. Instead, dollars could only be redeemed in large gold bars. However, until 1968 the U.S. Treasury stood ready to maintain the official dollar/gold rate in the free gold market of London and Zurich by purchasing dollars with gold should the gold price threaten to rise above $35. In that way the United States informally maintained a redeemable dollar at $35 an ounce for foreign individuals and firms as well as officially for governments and central banks. As European pressure for redemption assaulted the inflated dollar, however, the United States, in 1968, sealed off the dollar from the free gold market, establishing the short-lived "two-tier" gold market. In 1971 the last vestige of international gold redemption was ended by President Nixon, and the dollar became totally fiat.

The Spahr organizations advocated a return to the classic, pre-1933, gold coin standard, with gold coin circulating as the standard money. But they sidestepped the problem of considering the proper dollar weight by simply urging the definition of the gold dollar at 1/35 a gold ounce. Their major argument was that 35 dollars to the ounce was the existing legal definition, and that this definition was effectively the redemption rate for foreign governments and central banks. (They might have added, as we have seen, that $35 was also the effective redemption rate for foreign individuals.)

The sole basis of the Spahr call for $35 was that definitions, once selected, must stand forevermore. But this stance was a weak one, considering that there was no gold standard domestically, and no gold coin redemption at all. Why stand courageously for cleaving to a gold standard at $35 an ounce, when nothing like a genuine gold standard has existed since 1933? Indeed, if the Spahr group had been consistent in wanting to maintain the old definition of the dollar, it would have urged a return to the last definition under a true gold standard, the pre-Rooseveltian $20 to the ounce.

The fact that none of the Spahr group so much as contemplated a return to $20 hinted at a growing realization that $35 and, a fortiori, $20, was no longer a viable weight, considering the inflation of money and prices that had proceeded steadily since the advent of World War II. The "classic" gold standard before 1933 was marked by a pyramiding of dollar claims upon a much smaller gold stock (specifically bank deposits upon bank notes and in turn upon gold). During and after World War II, the inflationary pyramiding directed by the Federal Reserve became ever more top-heavy, and a return to a $35-an-ounce dollar would have risked a massive deflationary contraction of money. For that reason, such dissident members of the Economists' National Committee as Henry Hazlitt, and other economists such as Michael Angelo Heilperin, Jacques Rueff, and Ludwig von Mises, began calling for return to gold at a "price" much higher than $35.[14]

At any rate, at the present time, even the weak argument for a definition of the dollar at $35 no longer exists. There is no gold standard left in any sense, and the existing "definition" of the value of gold as being $42.22 an ounce is clearly only an accounting fiction, and at radical variance from its value on the gold market. In a return to the gold standard, we would begin de novo, and with a clear slate. In that case, we must realize that there is no moral obligation involved in framing an *initial* definition, and that a new definition of the dollar should therefore be set at whatever figure is pragmatically the most useful. What definition we choose for the new gold dollar is then dependent on what sort of monetary system we would like to achieve, as well as on what definition would assure the easiest transition to that desired system.

Which Gold Standard?

Which definition we choose, then, depends on what kind of gold standard we would like to attain. At the very least, it must be a genuine gold standard, that is, the dollar must be tied to gold permanently at a fixed weight, and must be redeemable in gold coin at that weight. That rules out all forms of pseudo gold standards such as the 1933–1971 monetary system of the United States, or its subset, the Bretton Woods system of 1945–1971. It rules out, similarly, the pseudo gold standard advocated by the supply-side economists, who would go back to something like Bretton Woods. There would then be no gold coin redemption, and, even worse than Bretton Woods, which at least kept a fixed dollar weight in gold, the Federal Reserve would be able to manipulate the dollar definition at will, in attempting to fine tune the economy to achieve such macroeconomic goals as full employment or price level stability.

We could in fact return to the classical gold standard such as all major nations were on before World War I and the United States from the 1850s to 1933. The major advantages would be a return to fixity of weight and to genuine redeemability in gold coin. A classical gold standard would be infinitely superior to either the current or the Bretton Woods system. In this case the particular definition chosen would not matter very much, except that it should be much higher than $35 so as not to tempt an unnecessary and massive deflationary contraction that would, at the very least, turn public opinion away from the gold standard for decades to come. More important, the classical gold standard would return to the very same system that created boom-and-bust cycles and brought us 1929 and at least the first four years of the Great Depression. It would, in short, retain the Federal Reserve System, and its system of cartelized banking, special privilege, and virtually inevitable generation of inflation and contraction. Finally, while the ultimate monetary commodity, gold, would be supplied by the free market, the dollar would not be truly denationalized, and it would still be a creature of the federal government.

We can do much better, and there seems little point in going to the trouble of advocating and working for fundamental reform while neglecting to hold up the standard of the best we can achieve. If in our disillusionment with central banking, we call for abolition of the Federal Reserve and a return to some form of free banking, what route could we then take toward that goal? The closest approximation to a free banking-and-gold standard was the American economy from the 1840s to the Civil War, in which there was no form of central banking, and each bank had to redeem its notes and deposits promptly in gold. But in working toward such a system, we must realize that we now have a gold supply nationalized in the coffers of the Federal Reserve. Abolition of the Federal Reserve would mean that its gold supply now kept in Treasury depositories would have to be disgorged and returned to private hands. But this gives us the clue to the proper definition of a gold dollar. For in order to liquidate the Federal Reserve and remove the gold from its vaults, and at the same time tie gold to the dollar, the Federal Reserve's gold must be revalued and redefined so as to be able to exchange it, one for one, for dollar claims on gold. The Federal Reserve's gold must be valued at *some* level, and it is surely absurd to cleave to the fictitious $42.22 when another definition at a much lower weight would enable the one-for-one liquidation of the Federal Reserve's liabilities as well as transferring its gold from governmental to private hands.

Let us take a specific example. At the end of December 1981, Federal Reserve liabilities totaled approximately $179 billion ($132 billion in Federal Reserve notes plus $47 billion in deposits due to the commercial banks). The Federal Reserve owned a gold stock of 265.3 million ounces. Valued at the artificial $42.22 an ounce, this yielded a dollar value to the Federal Reserve's gold stock of $11.2 billion. But what if the dollar were defined so that the Federal Reserve's gold stock equaled, dollar for dollar, its total liabilities—that is, $179 billion? In that case, gold would be defined as equal to $676 an ounce, or, more accurately, the dollar would be newly defined as equal to, and redeemable in 1/676 gold ounce. At that new weight, Federal Reserve notes would then be promptly redeemed, one for one, in gold coin, and Federal Reserve demand deposits would be redeemed in gold to the various commercial banks. The gold would then constitute those banks' reserves for their demand deposits. The abolition of Federal Reserve notes need not, of course, mean the end of all paper currency; for banks, as before the Civil War, could then be allowed to print bank notes as well as issue demand deposits.

This plan, essentially the one advocated by Congressman Ron Paul (R.-Texas), would return us speedily to something akin to the best monetary system in U.S. history, the system from the abolition of the Second Bank of the United States and the pet banks, to the advent of the Civil War. Inflation and business cycles would be greatly muted, if not eliminated altogether. Add the abolition of the Federal Deposit Insurance Corporation, the requirement of instant payment of demand liabilities on pain of insolvency, and the long overdue legalization of interstate branch banking, and we would have a system of free banking such as advocated by many writers and economists.

We could, however, go even one step further. If we were interested in going on to 100 percent reserve banking, eliminating virtually all inflation and all bank contraction forevermore, we might require 100 percent banking as part of a general legal prohibition against fraud. The substantial

100 percent gold reserve tradition (held by writers and economists rang-
ing from David Hume, Thomas Jefferson, and John Adams, and partly to
Ludwig von Mises), considers the issuing of demand liabilities greater
than reserves as equivalent to a warehouse issuing and speculating in
warehouse receipts for nonexisting deposits. In short, a fraudulent violation of bailment.

How might the United States go over to a 100 percent gold system? At
the end of December 1981, total demand liabilities issued by the entire
commercial banking system (that is, M-1), equaled $445 billion (including
Federal Reserve notes and demand, or rather checkable, deposits). To go
over immediately to 100 percent gold, the dollar would be newly defined at
1/1,696 gold ounce. Total gold stock at the Federal Reserve would then be
valued at $445 billion, and the gold could be transferred to the individual
holders of Federal Reserve notes as well as to the banks, the banks' assets
now equaling and balancing their total demand deposits outstanding. They
would then be automatically on a 100 percent gold system.

From the standpoint of the free market, there is admittedly a problem
with this transition to 100 percent gold. For the Federal Reserve's gold would
be transferred to the commercial banks up to the value of their demand
deposits by the Federal Reserve's granting a free gift of capital to the banks
by that amount. Thus, overall, commercial banks, at the end of December
1981, had demand deposits of $317 billion, offset by reserves of $47 billion.
A return to gold at $1,696 an ounce would have meant that gold transferred
to the banks in exchange for their reserve at the Federal Reserve would *also*
have increased their reserves from $47 to $317 billion, via a writing up of
bank capital by $270 billion. The criticism would be that the banks scarcely
deserve such a free gift, deserving instead to take their chances like all other
firms on the free market. The rebuttal argument, however, would stress that,
if a 100 percent gold requirement were now imposed on the banks, their free
gift would do no more than insure the banking system against a potential
holocaust of deflation, contraction, and bankruptcies.[15]

At any rate, whichever of the last two paths is chosen, money and
banking would at last be separated from the state, and new currencies,
whether "Hayeks" or "ducats," would be free to compete on the market
with the gold dollar. I would not advise anyone, however, to bet their life
savings on any of these proposed new currencies getting anywhere in this
competitive race.

Notes

1. The exception was the period 1896–1914, when a mild chronic inflation
(approximately 2 percent per year) resulted from unusual gold discoveries, in
Alaska and South Africa.

2. With the exception of the United Staes, which entered the war in the spring of 1917, two and a half years after the other belligerents. But even the United States went informally off the gold standard by prohibiting the export of gold for the duration of the war.

3. In olden days, the paper tickets were issued by the central government's Treasury (e.g., Continentals in the American Revolutionary war, *assignats* during the French Revolution, greenbacks during the American Civil War). Nowadays, in a more complex variant of the system, the tickets constituting the monetary "standard" are issued by the government's central bank.

4. Note that we are assuming that standard paper is legal tender, as indeed all government money now is. (That is, all creditors are compelled to accept the paper tickets in payment for money debt.) In our hypothetical scenario, all individual tickets marked "dollars" or "francs" would similarly possess legal tender power.

5. See, in particular, F. A. Hayek, *The Denationalisation of Money* (London: The Institute of Economic Affairs, 1976).

6. For his regression theorem, see Ludwig von Mises, *The Theory of Money and Credit*, 2nd ed. (New Haven, Conn.: Yale University Press, 1953), pp. 170–86. Also see Murray N. Rothbard, *The Case for a 100 Percent Gold Dollar* [1962] (Washington, D.C.: Libertarian Review Press, 1974), pp. 10–11.

7. We might apply to Hayek's scheme the sardonic words of the nineteenth-century French economist Henri Cernuschi, which Mises approvingly cited in a slightly different context: "I want to give everybody the right to issue banknotes so that nobody should take banknotes any longer." Ludwig von Mises, *Human Action* (New Haven, Conn.: Yale University Press, 1949), p. 443.

8. Thus, the pound sterling originated, *pace* its name, as a definition of one pound weight of silver, and the dollar originated as an ounce coin of silver in Bohemia. Much later, the "dollar" became defined as approximately 1/20 of an ounce of gold.

9. In Luxemburg, *three* government currencies—those of France, West Germany, and Luxemburg itself—circulate side by side.

10. In fact, even Hayek's current "ducat" scheme incorporates a commodity-basket plan. His proposed bank would fine tune the supply of ducats so as to keep the "price level" in terms of ducats always constant.

11. For an outstanding philosophical critique of Fisher's commodity dollar, see the totally neglected work of the libertarian political theorist Isabel Paterson. Thus, Paterson writes:

> As all units of measure are determined arbitrarily in the first place, though not fixed by law, obviously they can be altered by law. The same length of cotton would be designated an inch one day, a foot the next, and a yard the next; the same quantity of precious metal could be denominated ten cents today and a dollar tomorrow. But the net result would be that figures used on different days would not mean the same thing; and somebody must take a heavy loss. The alleged argument for a "commodity dollar" was that a real dollar, of fixed quantity, will not always buy the same quantity of goods. Of course it will not. If there is no medium of value, no money, neither would a yard of cotton or a

pound of cheese always exchange for an unvarying fixed quantity of any other goods. It was argued that a dollar ought always to buy the same quantity of and description of goods. It will not and cannot. That could occur only if the same number of dollars and the same quantities of goods of all kinds and in every kind were always in existence and in exchange and always in exactly proportionate demand; while if production and consumption were admitted, both must proceed constantly at an equal rate to offset one another.

Isabel Paterson, *The God of the Machine* (New York: Putnam, 1943), p. 203n.

12. Specifically, the Coinage Act of 1792 defined the "dollar" as *both* a weight of 371.25 grains of pure silver and a weight of 24.75 grains of pure gold—a fixed ratio of 15 grains of silver to 1 grain of gold. This 15:1 ratio was indeed the world market ratio during the early 1790s, but of course the market ratio was bound to keep changing over time, and thus bring about the effects of Gresham's law. Soon an increased silver production led to a steady decline of silver, the market ratio falling to 15.75:1. As a result, silver coins flooded into the United States, and gold coins flooded out. Silver remained the sole circulating coinage, until the Jacksonians in 1834 successfully brought back gold by debasing the gold weight of the dollar to 23.2 grains, lowering the weight by 6.26 percent. At this new ratio of 16:1, gold and silver circulated side by side for two decades, when the discovery of new gold mines in California, Russia, and Australia, greatly increased gold production, and sent the market ratio down to 15.3:1. As a result, gold coin poured in and silver flowed out of the country. The United States continued on a de facto gold monometallic standard, but a de jure bimetallic standard from the 1850s, with the market ratio holding at about 15.5:1 while the official mint ratio was 16:1.

By 1872, however, a few knowledgeable officials at the U.S. Treasury realized that silver was about to suffer a huge decline in value, since the European nations were shifting from a silver to a gold standard, thereby decreasing their demand for silver and increasing their demand for gold, and because of the discovery of the new silver mines in Nevada and other Mountain states. To keep the de facto gold standard, the Treasury slipped bills through Congress in 1873 and 1874, discontinuing the minting of any further silver dollars, and ending the legal tender quality of silver dollars above the sum of $5. This demonetization of silver meant that, when, in 1874, silver began a rapid market ratio decline above 16:1 and finally to 32:1 in the 1890s, silver coins would not flow into the country and gold would not flow out. Finally, in 1900, the dollar was defined de jure solely in terms of gold, at 23.22 grains.

See Ron Paul and Lewis Lehrman, *The Case for Gold* (Washington, D.C.: Cato Institute, 1982), pp. 17–19, 30–32, 60–66, 100–2.

13. In the United States, the Treasury holds the gold in trust for the Federal Reserve Banks at its depositories at Fort Knox and elsewhere.

14. These dissidents were virtually all in the Austrian tradition, and the three names in the text were all either students or followers of Ludwig von Mises.

In the light of later developments in the gold market, it is amusing to note that the Rueff–Hazlitt proposals for a gold dollar at $70 were scorned by virtually all economists as absurdly high, and that before 1968, monetarists and Keynesians alike were unanimous in predicting that if ever the dollar were cut loose from gold, the gold price would fall precipitately to its nonmonetary level, then estimated at approximately $9 per ounce. It is equally amusing to consider that most of these economists would still subscribe to the motto that "science is prediction."

15. On the paths to a genuine gold standard, see Murray N. Rothbard, *The Mystery of Banking* (New York: Richardson and Snyder, 1983), pp. 254–69. On the 100 percent gold tradition, see ibid., Rothbard, *Case*, and the neglected work by Mark Skousen, *The 100% Gold Standard: Economics of a Pure Money Commodity* (Washington, D.C.: University Press of America, 1977). Also see Rothbard, "Gold vs. Fluctuating Fiat Exchange Rates," in H. Sennholz, ed., *Gold Is Money* (Westport, Conn.: Greenwood Press, 1975), pp. 24–40.

2
The Monetary Writings
of Carl Menger

Hans F. Sennholz

A founder of a scientific system cannot be expected to develop his system in all details. His strength and lifetime may be insufficient to develop all implications and conclusions. He may prepare the blueprint and erect a few pillars that will support the structure. He may even give a great deal of care to a few details. But even the greatest mind must be content with a system that contains many cursory thoughts and unproven parts. He must rely on scholars who follow him to expand and complete the task.

Carl Menger was such a founder who in many respects resembled that great builder of classical economic thought, Adam Smith. In more or less modified form both systems of thought continue to exercise influence on contemporary economic thinking. Both were rejected by some thinkers, modified and criticized by others. Some used parts of the system as foundations on which they built magnificent superstructures; others have used them as points of departure to build theories of their own.

Carl Menger's *Grundsätze der Volkswirtschaftslehre* (Principles of Economics, 1871) is one of the greatest tracts in economic literature.[1] Few books have had a comparable influence, not because it was widely read and loudly acclaimed, but because a few capable students and followers recognized its value and adopted its thought. In it Menger laid a solid foundation for the theory of subjective value and a theory of the origin of money. He did not formulate many distinct theories in the book, but his brilliant observations there served as the cornerstones for many theories to come.

A few years later Menger published his second great work, which in its field was as significant as the *Grundsätze*. He aroused the interest of the academic world and the anger of the German Historical School with his *Untersuchungen über die Methode der Sozialwissenschaften und der politischen Oekonomie insbesondere* (Inquiries into the Method of the Social Sciences and Particularly Political Economy, 1883). This essay started the "battle of the century," commonly called the *Methodenstreit* (controversy on method).

Both works are landmarks in the history of economic thought. Both were translated in a number of other languages and are available to students of economics everywhere. But little is known about Menger's later monetary writings, which helped to bring currency reform and sounder money to Austria. Between 1889 and 1893 Menger published seven essays on monetary theory and currency reform that rank among the outstanding works on the subject matter. They are available only in the German language, which has seriously limited their influence on contemporary economic thought.

In the order of their publication Menger's monetary writings include the following:

"Die Kaufkraft des Guldens österreichischer Währung" (The Purchasing Power of the Austrian Guilder), 1889

"Geld" (Money), 1892, 2nd revised edition 1909

"Beiträge zur Währungsfrage" (Contributions to the Currency Issue), 1892

"Der Uebergang zur Goldwährung" (Transition to a Gold Currency), 1892

"Aussagen in der Valutaenquete" (Testimony before the Currency Commission), 1892

"Von unserer Valuta" (On Our Currency), 1892

"Das Goldagio und der heutige Stand der Valutareform" (The Gold Premium and the Present Currency Reform), 1893

On the Origin of Money

In this *Principles* Carl Menger had already sketched an irrefutable theory of the origin of money. He had dealt with it as a great thinker would deal with an important thought that deserves further scrutiny. In just a few pages he had presented an explanation of the origin of money, had enumerated "the kinds of money appropriate to particular peoples and to particular historical periods," had refuted the notion of money as a "measure of price," and described the development of coinage systems. But in *Principles* he did not proceed to the central problem of money, which is its exchange value, commonly called its purchasing power. He did announce "the theory of money," which is the very title of his chapter on money, but he actually developed only a brilliant theory of the *origin* of money.

Carl Menger refuted the doctrines so popular throughout the ages that indirect exchange and money are the products of authoritarian decree or social covenant. Plato had defined money as "an agreed-upon token for barter," and Aristotle had found that money was a product of agreement and law. Menger demonstrated, instead, that it is the unintended result of individual efforts of members of society. Every single individual is interested in exchanging less marketable goods for those of greater marketabilty, durability, and divisibility. Man's search for more marketable goods in time leads him to the most marketable good, which may also be the most durable, divisible, and transportable good known to him. Without any agreement, without legislative compulsion, in fact, even without any consideration of public interest and the public good, individuals are pursuaded to exchange their goods and services for more marketable goods, even if they are not needed for immediate use. The economic good that emerges as the most marketable good of all is called "money."

In his great essay on money,[2] which he completed more then twenty years later, Menger embarked upon a more systematic investigation into the nature of money. Once again his analysis led him toward a theory of the origin of money that openly contradicted the statist and socialist doctrines of his day. They credited the state with the "invention" of money and assigned its regulation and control to government. According to Menger, however, it is an irrefutable fact that individuals are eager to acquire money not by orders of their government, but in order to exchange it later for other economic goods. It is this conduct of individuals that is making certain goods the media of exchange.

In Menger's time many writers were eager to add secondary functions to that of medium of exchange. They spoke of money facilitating credit transactions or transmitting value through time and space. Or they dwelt on money as a general medium of payment. But Menger showed convincingly that all secondary functions can be deduced from the function of money as common medium of exchange. A credit transaction, after all, is merely an exchange of a present good for a future good. To be a transmitter of value through time and space depends on special suitability of a good for hoarding and shipping, which adds marketability and therefore enhances a good's qualification as medium of exchange.

On the Demand for Money

Carl Menger did not formulate a complete theory of the value of money, but the germs of almost all later doctrines and theories are more or less recognizable in his essay on money. His primary task was to explode many errors and fallacies that were leaving their mark not only on monetary thought but also on government policies. Above all, he sought to counter the growing trend toward holistic and collectivistic considerations by tracing all phenomena back to the actions of individuals. In all his investigations he sought to apply his subjective value theory and emphsize its importance for the elucidation of economic phenomena.

Throughout the history of economic thought many writers argued for the largest possible quantity of money. Others sought to enumerate objective factors that allegedly determine the demand for money. They suggested that the demand for money was determined by the quantity of exchangeable goods available in an economy, or by the volume of payments that need to be made. Others yet continue to speak of the velocity of circulation as a significant factor that influences the demand for money. All such explanations, according to Menger, are missing the mark. A realistic theory of the demand for money must be based on the monetary demand of individuals or groups of individuals who comprise a national economy. Their demand is the ultimate gauge of the national demand. In Menger's own words:

> The monetary demand of a national economy is the sum of the moneys needed by individuals and groups of individuals participating in the division of labor. It is a quantity the significance of which is visible not only in the aggregate, but also in the distribution among individuals. But the national demand is not a mere summation of the cash demand of individuals. We must consider also the services of financial institutions that substitute their instruments for cash or at least economize the use of cash.[3]

There is a demand for money because people want to hold some cash. They demand money in order to exchange it ultimately for other economic goods; they appraise it in the same way as they appraise all other economic goods. Their demand is reduced somewhat by institutions for the settlement of claims and counterclaims by mutual cancellation, such as clearinghouses. But such factors influence the demand for money only indirectly through their influence on people's desire for cash holdings.

Menger traced all monetary phenomena back to the choices and actions of individuals. He always took his stand against holistic concepts and notions. To him, it was a grievous error to calculate and make use of holistic concepts, such as total volume of trade, total quantity of money, general price levels, and velocity of national circulation. There are no objective factors creating a national demand; any and all factors affect individuals only as motivation.

The Purchasing Power of Money

It is an erroneous belief that money enters the market endowed with a given purchasing power independent of the valuations of individuals. Actually it receives its exchange value from the subjective valuations of all the persons exchanging goods and services in the market. But this exchange value appears to individuals as an accomplished fact, a given purchasing power, that must be accepted unconditionally. It is a given quantity of other economic goods that are offered for its acquisition. As the price of other goods and services is expressed in terms of money, so is the "price" of money—its purchasing power—expressed in the quantity of other goods that are offered for its acquisition. Several times Carl Menger announced a theory of the purchasing power of money. Several times he laid a solid foundation for such a theory but then failed to develop it in detail.

In his *Principles of Economics* Menger seemed to suggest that the value of money ultimately depends on the value of the material of which it is made. He offered a theory that explains the value of gold and silver coins from their potential use for industrial purposes. If for any reason the coins would lose their industrial usefulness they would also lose their purchasing power. Menger wrote:

> I refer to the observation that the character of money as an industrial metal often completely disappears from the consciousness of economizing men because of the smoothness of operation of our trading mechanism, and that men therefore only notice its character as a means of exchange. The force of custom is so strong that the ability of a metal used as money to continue in this role is assured even when men are not directly aware of its character as an industrial metal. This observation is entirely correct. But it is also quite evident that the ability of a material to serve as money, as well as the custom on which this ability is founded, would disappear immediately, if the character of money as a material applicable to industrial purposes were destroyed by some accident. I am ready to admit that, under highly developed conditions of trade, money is regarded by many economizing men only as a token. But it is quite certain that this illustration would immediately be dispelled if the character of coins as quantities of industrial raw materials were lost.[4]

His 1889 essay "The Purchasing Power of the Austrian Guilder" affirmed the same value theory, but under certain conditions also professed a kind of supply and demand theory that embodied elements of a quantity theory. He was greatly alarmed by the fact that the guilder's purchasing power exceeded the metal value of the silver guilder, which to him was an "economic anomaly" harboring "the greatest dangers to the Austrian economy."

Since 1879 the guilder had traded considerably above the value of the silver contained in the guilder. Menger explained this discrepancy as "rarity value" which came into existence when the government closed the mint. The market price of silver bullion had been falling throughout the 1870s, which in time would have caused the purchasing power of the guilder to fall to its bullion value. To take advantage of the lower silver cost, the people would have taken more silver to the mint to convert bullion to coins. But government intervened by closing the mint. "Free silver coinage would have prevented the discrepancy between the value of bullion and coinage," Menger explained. It would have kept the guilder's purchasing power at par with its silver value. But "under the present, artificially created conditions, the purchasing power of the Austrian guilder is determined by the relationship between the circulating media and the public demand for such media."[5]

Menger viewed the "rarity value" of money with great alarm. "There cannot be any doubt," he warned his readers, "that since 1879 the guilder's purchasing power has been subjected to continuous fluctuations." It is affected by every change in economic activity, in fact, inversely affected as money with ficticious value will neither enter nor leave the country and therefore escape the "regulatory influence of unlimited coinage."

In his 1892 "Contributions to the Currency Issue" Menger added four more "evils" and "dangers." First, the peculiarities of the Austrian monetary order cause the exchange rates between guilders and foreign currencies to fluctuate continually, which prevents reliable calculation for foreign trade and commerce. They turn all foreign trade into currency speculation and make all sales a "double business." Second, an artificial monetary system always faces the danger of a sudden resumption of coinage, which, in this case, would lower the guilder's objective exchange value and seriously disrupt financial markets. As the suspension of coinage was ordered without benefit of law or even regulation, it may be resumed at any moment. Third, an artificial currency is rather vulnerable to all kinds of crisis, which may cause it to fall to new discounts not only toward gold but even toward silver. And fourth, it is probably the greatest danger that silver prices can be expected to fall further and thus cause the discrepancy between the purchasing power of the silver guilder and its precious metal value to widen even further. It would render the Austrian currency system ever more precarious.[6]

Menger's concern about the "anomality" of the Austrian currency undoubtedly reflected his great anxiety about the total dependence of the Austrian national bank and its currency issues on the state. Again and again the Austrian government had used the bank to finance budgetary deficits and market its treasury obligations. Even after it had closed the mint in 1879, it had continued to manufacture silver guilders for its own account. In short, its repeated interventions had caused a separation of the guilder's purchasing power from its metallic base. In Menger's own words, purchasing power was "floating in mid-air" and, "in the true sense of the word, was reflecting an original rarity value brought forth by genuine and relatively severe rationing of our currency."[7]

Professor Menger, of course, was describing the fiat standard that causes the purchasing power of money to "float in mid-air." That is, the objective exchange value of money is determined by demand and supply— in the same way as the exchange ratios between other marketable goods are determined. In this sense his "float theory" becomes a "quantity theory" that points the way toward a modern theory of money. He placed the theory of money on a new foundation, the subjective value theory. But he did not have the opportunity or inclination to analyze the various determinants of the objective exchange value of money. He offered no explanation of the process of value determination at any given time and place.

Menger left this task to Friedrich von Wieser and Ludwig von Mises. The former elaborated the problem in a brilliant essay on the value of money and developed some determinants, especially the historical elements.[8] The latter presented a complete subjective theory of the value of money in his 1912 treatise *Theorie des Geldes und der Umlaufsmittel* (The Theory of Money and Credit).[9]

The Gold Standard

For Menger the pending currency reform made extreme demands on his time and strength. It made the year 1892 probably the most productive year in terms of literary effort and output. In January and February he published a series of articles "On Our Currency" in the *Allegemeine Juristen Zeitung* (General Journal for Jurists). On March 15 and 17 he testified before the Currency Commission that was meeting in Vienna.[10] In June his "Contributions to the Currency Issue," which had first appeared in the *Jahrbücher für Nationaloekonomie und Statistik*,[11] were republished as a separate booklet of fifty-nine pages by an eminent publisher, Gustav Fischer, in Jena. In the same month Menger released a thirty-six-page essay on the problems of "Transition to a Gold Currency" with Wilhelm Braumüller in Vienna and Leipzig. All these efforts sought to guide Austrian policymakers in their stated objective to reform the currency system and adopt the gold standard.

To Menger the gold standard was the ideal standard for civilized nations. In his "Contributions to the Currency Issue" he waxed eloquently on the evils of the "limping silver standard" and the great merits of a gold standard:

It is no coincidence that the civilized nations are striving universally and urgently to introduce a gold currency. Gold is the money of advanced nations in the modern age. No other money can provide the convenience of a gold currency in our age of rapid and massive commodity exchanges. Silver has become a troublesome tool of trade. Even paper money must yield to gold when it comes to monetary convenience in everyday life. A ten- or five-guilder gold coin would be more convenient than our ten- or five-guilder note. Moreover, under present conditions only a gold currency constitutes hard money. Neither a bank note and treasury note nor a silver certificate can take the place of gold, especially in moments of crisis.

The historic trend toward the formation of large states and markets has given additional impetus to gold as medium of exchange. In larger countries silver cannot even mediate satisfactorily domestic trade. International trade, which must not be restricted artificially, is growing in significance and dependence on gold. It also forces small countries to join larger trade areas and adopt gold as a medium of exchange. The international balance of payments of modern countries can only be settled in gold. Gold is the money of the world in our age; silver is the money of second-class countries only. Especially since the most important trading countries are using gold, no progressive society can cling to silver without becoming isolated—like an economic island in international commerce. We are accustomed to view economic problems from every conceivable angle except that given by their very nature and substance. Therefore, it is all the more important to emphasize that gold is the right medium of exchange for our age, not because it serves the interests of certain groups, but because it renders the services of money in a most useful, secure, and expedient manner.[12]

Menger did not overlook the technical and economic advantages of a gold currency, such as inexpensive minting, difficult counterfeiting, little wear and tear, greatest convenience, and easy transport. Above all, gold was the money of Austria's neighbors and trade partners, and the gold standard the only standard that offered full parity of the Austrian currency with other currencies.

Menger exerted a powerful influence on Austrian economic affairs. After all, he was the most celebrated Austrian economist, who a few years earlier had engaged the German economists in the heated *Methodenstreit* (dispute on method) from which he had emerged with great honor and acclaim. Moreover, he had been the tutor to the eighteen-year-old crown prince of Austria, the ill-fated Archduke Rudolf. In 1892, the year of the currency reform, Menger's voice was heard throughout the land, expounding and illustrating the merits of the gold standard. But he did not hesitate to point to two important problems which the currency commission had simply ignored: the general worldwide tendency of gold to appreciate in exchange value and the further rise of this exchange value as a result of the Austrian currency reform.

Menger rejected the old argument of the opponents of the gold standard that the quantity of newly mined gold in time will be insufficient to meet the growing needs of business, that the gold standard lacks the needed flexibility in the supply of money and, therefore, will cause serious shortages of money. In reality, as Menger pointed out, a growing relative scarcity of gold will raise the exchange value of gold and the purchasing power of every gold coin. "Surely, even if all the fears of declining gold production should come to pass, gold coins will not lose their function as media of exchange, but rather serve it ever more conveniently as their purchasing power continues to rise."[13]

To dispel the popular fear that the world will run out of gold and that its purchasing power is bound to soar, which would cause goods prices to fall, Menger cited the estimates of the U.S. director of the mint, a Mr. Leech, according to whom the low point of world gold production of less than 5 million ounces annually was reached in the years 1881 to 1885. Thereafter production began to rise again and exceeded 5.6 million ounces in 1890. Menger also called attention to the rising gold production in South Africa, where 65,000 ounces were mined in 1885, 220,000 ounces in 1888, 400,000 ounces in 1889, 500,000 ounces in 1890, and more than 750,000 ounces in 1891.[14] Of course, he could not foresee that South Africa was about to become the most important gold-producing country, which in time would "inflate" the world with gold at a production rate of more than 30 million ounces per year. Gold mining in other countries would add another 15–17 million ounces annually.

Menger was greatly concerned about the possible rise of the purchasing power of gold as a result of the Austrian currency reform. "No reasonable and knowledgeable observer of the situation can guarantee that the Austrian currency reform, even with most careful execution, will not bring about a considerable rise in the value of gold," he wrote.[15] It may cause goods prices to decline throughout the gold standard countries, cause wage rates to fall, and above all, change all creditor–debtor relationships to the benefit of creditors and the detriment of debtors. There could be evil consequences that must be avoided through careful planning and orderly transition to a gold currency.

To avoid a sudden rise in gold value as a result of new Austrian gold demand, Menger recommended a number of policy measures that, at least during a lengthy period of transition, would reduce the individual demand for gold. He favored the issue of subsidiary silver coins or notes fully backed by silver but also redeemable in gold, issue of smaller denomination bank notes, permission of note-issuing banks to hold part of their reserves in silver, no minting of small denomination gold coins, establishment of an international clearinghouse, further development of savings banks and savings associations, of the deposit system transferring deposits by checks, and other credit and clearing organizations. Such measures would allow the major nations gradually to enjoy the benefits of the gold standard without aggravating the danger of rising gold value. Having given due care and consideration of the interests of other countries on the gold standard, Menger claimed the right to acquire gold and proceed with the currency reform. After all, "it seems to be an impermissible and hopeless undertaking to assign to some civilized countries the role of second-class countries in monetary affairs," he observed.[16]

Testifying before the Currency Commission

In the spring of 1892, the secretary of the Austro-Hungarian treasury, Dr. Steinbach, invited Menger and other experts to testify before his committee and especially comment on the following questions:

1. What should be the standard of the currency system?
2. If it should be gold, should a quantity of silver coins be permitted, and what quantity?
3. Should it be permissible to issue a quantity of fully redeemable, non–interest-bearing treasury notes, and under what conditions?
4. What should be the ratio of conversion of the silver guilder to gold?
5. What should be the currency unit?[17]

In his lengthy testimony Menger again pointed at the great evils of the then current system, the speculative nature of all foreign trade, the isolation of Austrian financial affairs from the world market, the permanent pressure on Austrian prices, and permanently higher interest rates. But the worst evil and "central issue to the currency problem", according to Menger, was the great discrepancy between the guilder and its silver content, which he estimated at 20 percent. "The government of Austria-Hungary is in the position, by mere executive order, to reduce the real value of all obligations by one-fifth and give instant relief to all debtors.... In fact, every secretary of the treasury can reduce the wealth of a great many citizens by 20 percent."[18] Moreover, the purchasing power of the guilder may fall even further on account of the "irrational circulation of 312 to 412 million guilders of treasury notes," which may lead to a silver premium and note discount; altogether, many citizens of Austria-Hungary were facing the real danger of losing nearly 50 percent of their real wealth.[19] Therefore, in answer to the first question, Menger recommended adoption of the gold standard. But he urged the government to proceed most carefully and deliberately lest it disrupt the international gold market and cause the purchasing power of gold to rise. Currency redemption should commence only after years of thorough preparation when government should acquire the needed quantity of gold without disrupting or disturbing the precious metals markets.

To the second question, on the desirability of a quantity of silver coins under a gold standard, Menger had a ready answer: "A good silver currency presents no danger, for it replaces gold coins from which it receives its value."[20] Great dangers to the gold standard only arise from excessive issues of silver coins. The situation is explained by two basic economic principles pertaining to money: Gresham's law, according to which bad money crowds out a corresponding quantity of good money if both must be exchanged at faulty exchange rates, and the principle of monetary substitution, according to which good money serving as the common medium of exchange confers value on bad money that is fully redeemable in the former. Gold determines the value of silver money circulating beside it as long as the latter is present only in strictly limited quantities.

Menger sounded like a politician speaking to fellow politicians on the Currency Commission. Three distinct thoughts seem to permeate his testimony: the desirability of the gold standard for his country, his deep concern about potential disruptions of the international gold market as a result of Austria-Hungary's adoption of the gold standard, and his effort to make the transition as palatable and simple as possible. Seeking to convince his countrymen that the gold standard was within their reach, he pointed out that the standard prevalent was "gold-plated." But although the European currencies were gold-plated, Menger said,

> We must not scorn them. Money is no luxury. A gold-plated item at first renders the same services as genuine items as long as the plating is solid. If a gold currency is plated so solidly that it can survive the corrosive acid of a commercial crisis or even the ordeal of a war, then nothing can be said against it. In its center is a nucleus of solid paper, covered by a layer of subsidiary coins, covered by yet another thin layer of silver coins, and finally, over it all, a solid layer of gold. If we keep it that way we have a very useful gold currency. There are no pure gold currencies in Europe, only gold-plated currencies, even in England. Let us not be too demanding.[21]

Menger answered the third question in a similar manner: There is no basic objection to the emission of government obligations and their use as money as long as the quantity remains relatively small. But government obligations encounter great distrust, which cannot be surprising in the light of their sad history in Austria-Hungary. Therefore its quantity must be strictly limited to no more than 90 to 100 million guilders, which would amount to some 10 percent of government revenues. The notes must be redeemable at any time, but not be granted the quality of legal tender. In Menger's own words,

> The prompt redeemability of treasury notes in cash at the central treasury and, if possible, at all other public treasuries, may not only strengthen the fickle confidence of the people, but also serve effectively to limit their emission to the needed quantity. No objection can be raised from a technical financial point of view to regular emissions of some 90 to 100 million guilders that are fully redeemable on demand.[22]

For the same reason Menger even defended the issue of small denomination treasury notes: "As far as their acceptability and usage are concerned, I can see no danger in the emission of small, always redeemable notes, that is, five-guilder notes or even a certain quantity of one-guilder notes."

The fourth question, concerning the conversion ratio, was, according to Menger, a question of justice. We must create a *just* guilder that does not shift individual wealth, inflicting losses on some people and granting profits to others. In a currency reform the owner of present money must receive such quantities of gold money as he would be able to buy on his own in the moment of currency reform. All exchanges, therefore, should pursue the principle of "present rate," which is the only fair rate.

The same principle must apply also to the conversion of debt stated in old currency to debt denominated in new currency. The "present rate" is the only just conversion ratio. Menger rejected expressly the proposal that any debt conversion should be mindful of the exchange rate that existed at the time the debt was incurred. Future changes of exchange rates may be considered, but past changes in the purchasing power of money must not be taken into account in the conversion. He testified:

> The debtor who on January 1, 1862, incurred a debt of 1,000 guilders owes his creditor 1,000 guilders of present value. I do not deny that money, like all other goods, is subject to value changes. Its purchasing power is changing. Thirty years ago a guilder had more or less purchasing power. But this fact is ignored in legislation as well as in every-day life. He who owes 1,000 guilders and can only repay 999 guilders can be thrown into bankruptcy. But he who pays his creditor 1,000 guilders that in the meantime have lost one-third of their purchasing power, discharges his obligation. I should like to add that we all are accustomed to ignore such changes in the purchasing power of money. Even such excellent bankers as you, gentlemen, prepare your annual balance sheets

without considering whether your capital has gained in purchasing power or whether it has lost.... Therefore, while we may consider future changes in purchasing power, we may ignore past changes in a conversion of old currency debt to new gold-currency debt.[23]

The last question, on the future currency unit, occasioned only a few comments by Menger. He opposed the thought of Austria-Hungary joining a German mark system or a French franc system. Such a union would generate extreme confusion and necessitate complicated exchange rate calculations. He favored the preservation of the old guilder as currency unit but recommended that a new half-guilder coin be added to the given coinage. He warned against two possible mint mistakes, to make coins either too large or too small for ready acceptance and use by the public. For him the present guilder was just right, an ideal unit for a gold currency.[24]

Errors of Reform

On August 2, 1892, a few months after Menger testified before the Currency Commission, the Austro-Hungarian government conducted the currency reform. It enacted an exchange rate of one guilder or two new crowns to 2.10027 French francs and announced gold redemption for January 1, 1896 or 1897, or possibly earlier. In an essay published in the *Bohemia* in June 1893, under the title "The Gold Premium and the Present Currency Reform," Professor Menger analyzed the reform and criticized the official blunders. Except for a minor essay on "Money and Coinage since 1857," in the *Oestereichische Staatswörterbuch*, in 1897, and except for the 1900 and 1909 editions of his famous essay on money, this work on the gold premium was to be his last on the subject matter of money. Thereafter, the genius reformer of classical economics and fearless knight of the *Methodenstreit* fell into silence as if he despaired about his country and the world.

Menger applauded the early successes of the reform. The currency act establishing the gold crown had hardly been passed when gold was entering the country. The conditions were most favorable as South African gold production was accelerating, lowering the exchange value of gold. But above all, the government of the United States was conducting inflationary policies that led to massive shipments of gold to Austria. More than half of the gold imports consisted of American eagles.[25]

But amid all the exuberance of success, a most disturbing factor began to make its appearance: Gold and foreign exchange rose to a 3 percent premium. All further gold acquisition had to be suspended and the reform interrupted because the guilder fell to a serious discount. The ultimate goal of reform, the beginning of redemption in gold, disappeared on the distant horizon.

The reason for this embarrassing development, according to Menger, had to be sought in a number of official blunders. The government had rushed to convert its funds into gold, which had greatly lifted the price of its obligations and substantially lowered their yield. In fact, silver obligations that are about to be converted to gold obligations tend to rise in price and their yields tend to fall, especially if silver is falling in value and gold is rising. In Austria-Hungary the public enthusiasm about the new gold currency caused interest rates to plummet, which soon surpassed all expectations and connections with Austrian reality. A reaction in the form of rising interest rates, rising gold prices, and falling guilder value became unavoidable.

The readjustment was all the more painful as Austrian obligations owned and held abroad experienced the same boom and bust. By 1893 many foreigners were selling their guilder holdings in Austrian markets, or were withdrawing their deposits, which depressed the guilder and lifted gold even further.

As soon as the gold premium made its appearance, Professor Menger insisted, the gold purchases should have been suspended. But the authorities did the very opposite. The purchases were continued with great haste. "In fact one could get the impression," Menger observed, "that the great and complicated reform work lacked consistent leadership, that everyone proceeded on his own account, the governments of both Austria and Hungary, the central bank, and the gold-purchase syndicate, that each one sought to excel the other in 'success stories.' Thereby all precautions were thrown to the wind."[26]

The purchases were conducted in great haste by various government authorities. But above all, the Austro-Hungarian Bank, which was the note-issuing central bank, bought most of the gold in the domestic market, thereby draining and depleting this market of gold and foreign exchange until it brought forth a gold premium and guilder discount. The bank bought gold for some 40 million guilders, thus releasing new bank credits through what later was to be called "open market purchases," thereby spreading fears of depreciation throughout the exchange markets. Therefore, it can hardly be surprising that the guilder fell to a discount.

To commence redemption of all notes in gold and thus return to sound money, Menger considered it an inescapable requirement to eradicate the gold premium and note discount. In his own words,

> For the present state of our currency it does not matter much whether we must calculate in guilders or half-guilders, in pennies or half-pennies,

whether we use convenient one-guilder notes or inconvenient under-valued silver guilders or silver crowns, whether we make change in silver or copper coins, or in nickel or bronze subsidiary coins, whether the gold is kept in this bank or shipped to that bank. But a serious and purposeful currency reform is not possible as long as domestic and foreign markets deny us the exchange rates on which we legally have embarked.[27]

Menger was always skeptical about the knowledge and wisdom of the political authorities that were conducting the reform. But he had an abiding faith in the principles and laws of the market that spring from the subjective choices and actions of men. If only the authorities would abstain from inflicting new harm on society, economic conditions would soon improve through adjustment and readjustment. In his words: "For a healing of the evil we must now wait for favorable conditions, for the gradual healing powers of natural forces that are effective also in economic life, but above all, for a careful treatment of domestic currency markets. That is to say, we must avoid those blunders that caused the evil.[28]

It would be a mistake to suppose that in his monetary writings Carl Menger developed a consistent theory of money and credit. That was not his intention; his primary concern was economic justice and social division of labor, which are basic to economic productivity and individual well-being. He was greatly concerned about the preservation of that polyglot state of the Hapsburgs, Austria-Hungary, which was uniting many peoples speaking different languages and leading them to live together harmoniously in one state. But to most of his countrymen the union was unwanted. They preferred national favors and privileges over peaceful cooperation, government authority over individual freedom, inflation and credit expansion over gold, and sound money. Their hopes and aspirations were to come to pass with the dissolution of the empire just twenty-five years later.

Carl Menger did not complete the splendid work he had begun in his youth. His great mind, which had found its own road and carried its own lamp, clearly recognized the destiny of mankind. He saw the inflations that were to ravish income and wealth, and the twentieth century wars in which human folly and tragedy were to reach their climax. Soon after the publication of his essays on money Carl Menger fell silent, perhaps despairing about the future of his beloved country and the fate of mankind.

Notes

1. Material from Carl Menger, *Principles of Economics*, reprinted by permission of New York University Press. Copyright © 1976 by Institute for Humane Studies.

2. Carl Menger, *The Collected Works of Carl Menger* (London: London School of Economics and Political Science, 1936), vol. 4, pp. 1–116.

3. Ibid., p. 114.

4. *Principles of Economics*, p. 320.

5. "The Purchasing Power of the Austrian Guilder," 1889, in *Collected Works*, vol. 4, p. 121.

6. "Contributions to the Currency Issue," in *Collected Works*, pp. 138–41.

7. Ibid., p. 138.

8. F. von Wieser, "Der Geldwert und seine geschichtliche Veranderungen," in *Zeitschrift fur Volkswirtschaft, Sozialpolitik und Verwaltung* 13 (1904).

9. Ludwig von Mises, *The Theory of Money and Credit* (New Haven, Conn.: Yale University Press, 1953), pp. 97–123.

10. "Testimony before the Currency Commission," Imperial Court and State Printing Office, 1892, pp. 197–223, 269–71, reprinted in *Collected Works*, vol. 4, pp. 225–86.

1!. 3rd series, vol. 3.

12. *Collected Works*, vol. 4, pp. 154, 155.

13. Ibid., p. 156, n. 1.

14. "Contributions to the Currency Issue," in *Collected Works*, p. 157.

15. Ibid., p. 167.

16. Ibid., p. 168.

17. "Testimony before the Currency Commission," *Collected Works*, vol. 4, p. 225 et seq.

18. Ibid., p. 228.

19. Ibid., p. 229.

20. Ibid., p. 246.

21. Ibid., p. 247.

22. Ibid., p. 244.

23. Ibid., pp. 256, 257.

24. Ibid., p. 269.

25. Ibid., p. 310. On July 14, 1890, the Sherman Act, pasing both houses of the U.S. Congress, provided that the U.S. Treasury purchase 4.5 million ounces of silver monthly, against which legal tender notes, redeemable in gold or silver coins at the discretion of the Treasury, would be issued.

26. Ibid., p. 320.

27. Ibid., p. 323.

28. Ibid., p. 324.

3
Ludwig von Mises and the Gold Standard

Richard M. Ebeling

I n the 1930s Lionel Robbins was once gently criticized by Oskar Morgenstern for creating a false impression of the Austrian school of economics to English-speaking readers. Morgenstern argued that in *The Nature and Significance of Economic Science* Robbins had represented "the Viennese economists...in certain important points as being much more of a school with uniform views than they really are."[1] What Morgenstern was alluding to was the fact that while those who we now classify as the interwar members of the Austrian school viewed themselves as sharing a common intellectual heritage coming from the earlier writings of Carl Menger, Eugen von Böhm-Bawerk, and Friedrich von Wieser, there was no unanimity among them concerning either the theoretical or policy implications of that heritage.[2] On the one hand, the Austrians stood as a cohesive group in their emphasis on methodological individualism, their focus on the subjectivist nature of the data of economic science and in their defense of a "causal-genetic" or process analysis of economic phenomena in opposition to the "functional" or equilibrium approach of the Lausanne school.[3] On the other hand, extensive and often heated debates were carried on within the school; among the questions in dispute were whether economics was an a priori or an empirical science, the role of psychological elements in the theory of value, the laws of imputation of value to factors of production, and the basis for the discount of future goods against present goods.

In matters of policy, unanimity was just as rare. In general the Austrian economists of the period shared a common belief in the relative superiority of the market as an institutional framework for economic coordination. But the school was far from any agreement as to the superiority of unadulterated laissez-faire. Among the senior members of the Vienna group only Ludwig von Mises can be considered to have argued a consistent case for classical liberalism and economic freedom. And to the extent that some of the younger members of the school came to support a more or less free market position on most policy issues it seems that it was mainly through Mises' influence.[4]

Monetary Theory and the Austrians

In monetary theory and policy there was also less than unanimous agreement among the Austrian economists, though here, again, the participants viewed themselves as beginning their discussions upon a common intellectual inheritance. In this instance the foundations were to be discovered, for the most part, in the earlier writings of Menger, Böhm-Bawerk, and Knut Wicksell. A common element in each of their contributions was an emphasis on analyzing economic and monetary processes in "individualistic" or disaggregated terms.

In his lengthy essay on money, "Geld," Menger criticized the mechanical transactions assumptions underlying the then prevailing concept of the velocity of circulation of money. Rather than beginning with the economy as a whole, Menger argued that the aggregate demand for money had to be constructed or built up from the individual demands for money, and the latter had to be understood in terms of choice-theoretic decisions concerning preferences for cash holdings in the face of uncertainty and speculation about the future.[5]

For the later Austrians a crucial aspect in Böhm-Bawerk's capital theory was its focus on the various relationships and interdependencies in the production processes. Production not only took time but involved a structure of complementary steps leading to the successful completion of finished goods. The temporal web of stages of production, within which decentralized production plans and activities were being undertaken, was held together and coordinated through the system of market prices and the rate of interest.[6]

Wicksell's importance was his demonstration of how a cumulative rise or fall in prices could be brought about through changes in the money rate of interest. What was significant in his exposition was his explanation of the mechanism by which a cumulative process could be set in motion *and* its effects on the various prices in the structure of production.[7] The cumulative rise or fall in prices was brought about through the emergence of a discrepancy between the money rate of interest, at which loans could be secured, and the anticipated rate of profit as perceived by potential borrowers in the market. A money rate below (or above) the "natural rate,"[8] however, was not neutral in its effects on various prices in the economy. The role of the rate of interest as a capitalization factor meant that a lowering (or raising) of the money rate of interest would enhance (or reduce) to a greater extent the expected profitability of long-term, as opposed to short-term, investments. In the cumulative process, while all prices would be rising (or falling) the effect would be relatively more intensive in those production processes that would be considered more "roundabout."[9]

The Work of Mises

These three strands of thought were brought together by Ludwig von Mises, first in *The Theory of Money and Credit* (originally published in 1912 and revised in 1924)[10] and in his monograph, *Monetary Stabilization and Cyclical Policy* (1928).[11] Using Menger's theory of the origin of money[12] and cash balance approach, Mises constructed a theory of the value of money that successfully incorporated the concept of marginal utility and broke out of the dilemma of the Austrian circle.[13] However, the explanation of a given value of money was only a preliminary step (albeit a theoretically important one) to the construction of a dynamic analysis of the process by which *changes* in the purchasing power of money occur in the market, an analysis which he attempted to construct in purely methodological individualistic terms.[14]

In the Misesian schema, effects of changes in the demand for or supply of money never manifest themselves simultaneously or immediately in all segments of the market. Any changes, whether in the demand for money or in its supply, always have their origin with changes in the circumstances of individual decisionmakers, either with a change in the desire for cash balances with the nominal quantity of money in the economy unchanged, or a change in the nominal quantity of money available to individuals with preferences for cash holdings unchanged, or a combination of the two. While the end result of such changes in individual circumstances was, for the economy as a whole, a rise or fall in the general purchasing power of money, this end result only emerged as the culmination of a sequential process through which each market participant came to be affected by the initial change in the monetary position of some individual(s). During this "transmission mechanism" relative prices and incomes were seen by Mises as being modified in ways that (potentially) had both temporary and permanent effects.

Money, therefore, was seen by Mises as necessarily and always nonneutral in its effects on the "real" economy. This was due to the fact that monetary expansions and contractions could work their effects upon the economic system only through changes in the monetary demand and supply positions of the individual transactors, who then transmitted their changed circumstances to others through modifications in their buying and selling patterns. As the impact of a monetary expansion (or contraction) came to be diffused through the economy, each step of the process would see changes in the relative demands for various products, bringing about changes in relative prices, the relative profitabilities of alternative production activities, and, therefore, the relative income positions of various individuals and groups in the economy. In Mises' eyes, it was only through this type of microeconomic "step-by-step" analysis of how monetary forces worked their effects upon the *structure* of relative prices that one could logically explain how a change in the demand or supply of money brought about a modification in the general *scale* of prices.[15]

It also highlighted the fact that money's "real effects" on an economy were not just its influence upon the level of total employment and output. Even if an economy was at "full employment," the process by which a monetary change was introduced into the system, and then sequentially came to be spread through the whole economy, would influence (at least for as long as the monetary change continued and had not worked its way through the entire system) the *real* pattern or allocation of production activities and the distribution of income. Any changes in total employment or output during a monetary expansion or contraction would themselves be one of the consequences of the (at least temporary) changes in the relative structure of prices and wages occurring as a result of the process by which changes in the general purchasing power of money emerged.[16]

Mises' theory of the trade cycle is an application to a particular case of his more general theory of the nonneutrality of money. More specifically it attempts to explain the process by which an expansion in the supply of credit (in excess of voluntary savings) through the loan market can bring about disproportional investment in the "higher stages of production" that in the course of the cycle will be found to be unsustainable (given the savings available in the economy as a whole). Mises carried out the exercise by combining Böhm-Bawerk's capital theory and Wicksell's interest rate mechanism with his own sequence analysis of monetary forces.

How changes in the quantity of money and credit would influence the direction and pattern of economic activities depended upon the point at which and the form in which the additional (or subtracted) sums were introduced into (or withdrawn from) the system. In the case of the trade cycle, Mises postulated that additional credits were in the form of producer loans. Assuming that prior to the credit expansion the rate of interest was one at which the loan market was in equilibrium,[17] additional demand for funds could be stimulated only by a lowering of the market rate which, in relation to the preceding equilibrium rate, would enhance the prospective profitability of various investment projects that earlier were viewed as too costly by potential borrowers. With savings decisions of ultimate income recipients assumed unchanged, borrowers who have taken up the additional credits begin new "roundabout" processes of production in excess of (in Böhm-Bawerkian terms) the subsistence fund available to sustain the factors of production during the production period.[18] The expenditures on new investment projects manifest themselves as increased demands for factors of production in the "higher orders" of the production structure.[19] Factor prices in these sectors of the economy tend to rise, changing the opportunity cost of alternative employments. Labor and complementary resources are drawn into these activities, either from alternative production uses or from the ranks of the unemployed.[20] As "higher order" expenditures are transformed into factor incomes, the consumption demand of those employed in the new occupations increase, tending over time to bring about a rise in the prices of finished goods. The rising prices for "lower order" consumption goods now reverse the relative profitability of alternative employment opportunities in the economy, tending to draw resources away from the "higher order" projects. If the credit expansion had been a single-injection phenomenon, Mises argued, the higher order projects begun would now either have to be abandoned because of the higher costs of their completion or the unavailability of complementary investments or, if completed, would have to operate at a rate of return less than initial expectations.[21]

However, if the credit expansion is continued and, particularly, continued at an increasing rate, an upward price-spiraling competitive race is set in motion between those who period after period receive the additional sums initially and attempt to maintain or draw additional factors of production into the more roundabout processes and those who later in the repeated sequential process experience increases in the demand for and prices of their products and attempt to retain or redirect resources back to less roundabout production activities. The process could only come to an end in one of two ways, Mises argued, either through a conscious decision on the part of the monetary authorities to halt the credit expansion or through a complete collapse of the monetary unit in a hyperinflation. But once the monetary expansion came to an end, an economic downturn was inevitable. The distortions in the structure of relative prices, the misdirections of resources among the higher orders of production and the relative income shares created by "forced savings" would all be found to be unsustainable with the removal of the monetary prop that had established and maintained them during the upturn.[22] An adjustment of relative prices, a reallocation of the factors of production among alternative uses and a shift in relative income shares would all be part of the prerequisites for a return to an economic situation consistent with the underlying pattern of consumer demands and time preference for present and future goods as they would now show themselves in an environment free from monetary influences.[23]

Mises' Theory of the Trade Cycle

Mises' theory of the trade cycle became the centerpiece around which Austrian discussions of monetary and cyclical phenomena revolved during

most of the interwar period. The most prominent expositor and elabora-
tor of the theory was Friedrich A. von Hayek,[24] who, along with Lionel
Robbins,[25] created an international recognition for the "Austrian Theory
of the Trade Cycle." Expositions and applications were also presented in
the 1930s by Gottfried Haberler,[26] Fritz Machlup,[27] and Erich Schiff.[28]
Richard Strigl, in a restatement of Böhm-Bawerk's capital theory, incorporated a version of the theory in his analysis of monetary influences on
the capital structure.[29] There were even right-wing and left-wing proponents of the theory in England. The former included, besides Robbins,
Frederic Benham[30] and H.F. Fraser[31] and, partly, T.E. Gregory.[32] The latter
group included M.A. Abrams,[33] E.F.M. Durbin,[34] and Hugh Gaitskell (who
later was a leader of the British Labour party).[35] In the United States, C.A.
Phillips, T.F. McManus, and R.W. Nelson used the Austrian theory as the
analytical framework for their economic history of the great depression.[36]
And the Austrian analysis was even integrated into a popular American
economics textbook of the late 1930s.[37]

The policy conclusions to be drawn from the Austrian theory of the
trade cycle, however, were far from uniform. On the left Abrams and
Durbin concluded that the theory demonstrated the instability of private
banking and capitalism in general, and therefore the necessity for state
central planning and nationalization of banking and credit institutions.
On the right Benham and Fraser argued for the British central bank to
return to a gold standard with institutional reforms that would enhance
wage flexibility and business competitiveness to lift the British economy
out of the depression and be responsive to future changes in economic
circumstances. Lionel Robbins, in the most lucid and eloquent of the
Austrian analyses of the Great Depression, also called for a return to the
gold standard under which the central banking authorities would play by
the international rules of the game in expanding and contracting the
domestic currency to reflect changes in the distribution of gold among
the nations of the world; but no rigid strait jacket was proposed, Robbins
believing at the same time that some discretionary authority should be
left in the hands of the central bank "to mitigate the instability of
business."[38]

Among the Austrians in the more narrow sense, discussions concerning the appropriate goals and methods for monetary policy centered
around the question of "neutral money." Wicksell had given different
definitions for the term, the "natural rate" of interest.[39] In some places he
used the term to mean that rate at which saving equaled investment. In
other places it was defined as the rate of interest at which a stable "price
level" was maintained. In the late 1920s and early 1930s, some of the
Austrian school economists attempting to use and extend the Wicksellian framework for purposes of business cycle analysis came to see a

contradiction between these two definitions.[40] Friedrich von Hayek, in particular, emphasized that in an economy experiencing increases in productivity that, ceteris paribus, would result in a declining price level due to the increasing output, a rate of interest sufficiently low to bring about an increase in the supply of money in circulation to keep the price level stable would be below that rate at which the demand for capital would be equal to the supply of savings in the economy. Hence, a policy of price level stabilization through the use of the interest rate mechanism could generate a discrepancy between saving and investment that might set in motion a cyclical process of the type described by Mises.[41]

If money had the potential for such destabilizing influences on the structure of production because of the nonneutral manner in which monetary injections could impinge upon the structure of intertemporal prices, then, Hayek concluded, the scientific question confronting monetary policy was how to "neutralize" money's effects on the relative prices of the economy. It was evident to Hayek that increases in the supply of money to compensate for productivity increases were both unnecessary and, in fact, inherently disruptive. However, circumstances did exist, Hayek said, in which changes in the money supply were justified to maintain monetary neutrality. These involved changes in the demand for money, specifically, changes either in the payment "habits" of the community or in the number of monetary transactions between the stages of production. Hayek, though, was extremely cautious in his prescriptions: The practical difficulty of instituting such a monetary policy arose from the microeconomic problem the central banking authority would have in seeing to it that the changes in the quantity of money were distributed to (or withdrawn from) those specific individuals experiencing changes in their demand for money. He concluded that possibly the only realistic system for the minimization of cyclical fluctuations was a 100 percent reserve gold standard under central bank supervision.[42]

Both Gottfried Haberler and Fritz Machlup drew similar conclusions about the rules for a policy of neutral money. A change in the price level, Haberler argued, could have its origins from either the money side or the goods side. In the former category, there was general agreement, he said, concerning the undesirable consequences of monetary expansions or contractions that brought about an absolute rise or fall in the price level. Absolute inflation was injurious, he stated, because by falsifying interest rate signals it set in motion capital investments in excess of savings, with an eventual economic crisis due to the disequilibrium relationships created by the credit expansion. Absolute deflation merely brought about a depression without a boom, a depression from which the economy would recover only when prices and wages had adjusted downward sufficiently to be consistent with the smaller quantity of money in the economy.

There still remained the question, Haberler said, of a relative inflation. By this he meant an increase in the quantity of money that just
counterbalanced changes on the goods side that in the absence of the
monetary expansion would have resulted in a lower price level. He distinguished between three types of changes from the goods side: changes
in the techniques of production, a lengthening of the processes of production, and an increase in population. In the first case, which represented an increase in productivity or output per head, a fall in prices was
not detrimental in that the greater outputs produced at lower costs and
sold at lower prices were planned for by the respective producers; while
the producers might err in failing to anticipate correctly the shape and
position of the respective demand curves they faced, this was a matter of
relative prices and not absolute prices. A monetary expansion to compensate for productivity increases would, as in the case of an absolute
inflation, distort the rate of interest and market prices with a resultant
misdirection of resources and an eventual depression. However, in the
latter two cases, Haberler argued, both a lengthening of the production
structure in which there occurred an increase in the number of times the
unfinished products changed hands before reaching the consumption
stage, and an increase in population with only a proportional increase in
the volume of production (output per head remaining constant) would
put unnecessary downward pressure on nominal wages and prices simply
because of an insufficiency of means of exchange to service the larger
number of transactions. Thus, a monetary accommodation to compensate for the latter two cases was justified. While the various index
numbers that could serve as a guide for a policy of neutral money might
be difficult to construct in terms of scientific precision, Haberler
believed it was possible to use less exact ones if done with caution.[43] He
did point out, however, that the institution of a national monetary policy
to neutralize money's influences on the "real" economy might be inconsistent with the maintenance and operation of an international gold
standard.[44]

Fritz Machlup made similar arguments: Falling prices due to productivity increases were not inherently destabilizing and any monetary
compensation, because of its influence on the rate of interest and the
structure of production, could only generate cyclical distortions. The
"proper limits" for monetary adjustment on the part of the central banking authorities were, he said: counteracting deflation resulting from
spontaneous hoarding, an increase in the number of households desiring
to hold cash balances and increases in the number of transactions steps
in the stages of production. However, like Hayek, Machlup was extremely
doubtful about the ability of the monetary authorities to introduce the
compensations in a manner that would not, in fact, bring about new
distortions in the economy.[45]

Not all of the Austrian economists shared this view concerning the limits of compensatory monetary policy. Alexander Mahr insisted that a policy of neutral money could retard economic growth. Firms experiencing increases in productivity and for whose products market demand was highly elastic would absorb an increasing share of the purchasing power of the buying public; revenues would decline in competing industries, slowing capital investment in those sectors, and any resistance to wage reductions by workers in these latter industries could generate increasing unemployment. Mahr concluded, therefore, that stabilization of the price level was preferable to a falling price level.[46]

Many of the Austrians in the interwar period, as we have seen, accepted Mises' reformulation and refinement of Wicksell's theory of the cumulative process as a logically satisfactory framework for understanding the emergence and phases of the business cycle. The problem of trying to neutralize monetary influences on the real economy led almost all of them to accept and endorse, *in theory*, an activist role for the central monetary authority. Their hesitation to advocate its implementation was due to the *practical* difficulties that were seen as insurmountable for the foreseeable future. The gold standard—albeit a cautiously managed one—was a second best to minimize the undesirable consequences from monetary disturbances. An unmanaged, privatized gold standard never seriously entered into their discussions.

Mises as Political Economist

While Mises' writings were the basis for much of the subsequent Austrian analyses of cyclical fluctuations, his own policy conclusions diverged radically from theirs. Unlike most of the other Austrian economists, Mises wholeheartedly and enthusiastically endorsed the gold standard as the most desirable monetary framework for a market economy. His reasons for doing so were both practical and theoretical, and both need to be understood to appreciate his grave doubts about government management of the monetary system and his forceful defense of a gold standard.

As a political economist, Mises viewed the gold standard as the only monetary system that potentially could free the determination of the purchasing power of money from the influence of government intervention.[47] Looking over the broad sweep of history, it was absolutely clear to him that the history of money was nothing less than one long tragic account of incessant state debasement of the monetary unit and an accompanying disruption of economic progress and social development. From the coin clipping of ancient kings and princes through the tidal waves of paper money inflations to the manipulative subterfuge of modern central banking, political influence or control over money and banking had brought in its train nothing but economic havoc and social conflict.[48]

Deceptions and delusions were behind this sorry course of events, Mises argued. From the first time a ruler debased the gold or silver content of the coinage that was either left in his custody or ordered into his vaults, inflation has been a deceptive method by which the political authority could garnish an additional portion of the citizenry's wealth without the blatant seizure of property or taxation of income. Inflation became a means for the imposition of a hidden tax that both enhanced the economic position of the state in the society and enabled the government to cultivate the impression among the populace that it, compared to all others in the community, possessed the magical powers to turn stones into bread. The state could produce benefits for all at a cost to none. But the lie in the fantasy, Mises insisted, was that what government gave to some it could only provide by taking from others. The state could *redistribute* wealth; it could not *create* it. It was precisely because of money's nonneutrality, that its full influences were only felt through time and not simultaneously in all segments of the market, that money creation could enhance the real incomes of some at the expense of others—those closest to the point of monetary injection being the early recipients of the additional sums of money.[49]

The second delusion, Mises said, was the confusion between money and capital. The arena in which savings was lent and borrowed had colloquially become known as the "money market." There arose from this the mistaken belief that interest rates were high because money was scarce and that the solution to high rates of interest was an expansion in the supply of money available for loans. But interest rates were what they were, Mises argued, not because of a lack of money but, rather, because of a scarcity of capital. The insufficiency of means in relation to desired ends imposed the requirement of choice upon human agents. Just as individuals had to allocate their scarce means among alternative uses in the present, they likewise were constantly having to make decisions on how to allocate those means available now among uses in the present and the future. The rate of interest was nothing more than the intertemporal price established by the higgling of the market between those who wished to use those present means here and now and those desiring to utilize them for purposes not coming to fruition until later. Monetary injections entering the money markets might have the capacity *temporarily* to lower the rate of interest and redistribute the available resources among different agents in the economy, but it could not necessarily create new capital. It was the very conclusion of Mises' theory of the trade cycle that misdirections of capital through such interest distortions could only lay the seeds for a future recession when the distribution of capital and labor among various types of investment projects came to be seen to be incompatible with the savings base upon which the society's production structure rested.[50]

Finally, the third delusion that Mises saw was the belief that the source of employment was the level of "effective demand" and that lapses from full employment could be corrected through sufficient increases in the total purchasing power in the economy. The first principle from which all economic reasoning begins is the existence of an insufficiency of means to achieve all the purposes agents would desire to attain. A denial of scarcity would be a denial of the need for either choice or economizing. It would imply a world in which the available means *exceeded* the ends they could serve. In such an environment no one would have to work, for there would be no work needing to be done, and the only dilemma facing *everyone* would be how to allocate leisure time among alternative entertainments. But in a world of scarcity there is always work to be done because there remain ends for which the means are still insufficient. Mises concluded, therefore, that the fundamental truth of Say's law remained intact: In a world of constant change, in which production today was guided by expectation about consumers' demands tomorrow, too much of some things and too little of others might be produced. But an overabundance of all things such that employment for all those desiring employment could not find it at some market-established structure of wages was logically impossible as long as there still remain unfulfilled human wants.[51] If an economy was suffering from prolonged high unemployment, the source lay not with deficient "aggregate demand" but rather with a pervasive disequilibrium in the structure of relative prices and wages that precluded the necessary adjustment in product and factor markets for a return to "full employment." The attempt to overcome such cost–price rigidities, Mises insisted, through the device of monetary expansion could succeed only for as long as prices rose while money wages remained constant or increased to a lesser degree. Only through "money illusion" could inflation succeed in bringing about a decline in the real cost of labor sufficient to bring about a return to full employment. As early as 1931, however, Mises argued that, in fact, trade unions were quite conscious of changes in real wages due to changes in the purchasing power of money and the likelihood of their long-term passivity at the bargaining table in an inflationary environment was not to be expected.[52] The pursuit of full employment via the printing press could only set in motion an upward spiral of wage demands on the part of the unions and an ever increasing monetary expansion to compensate for the unemployment caused by the capture of real wages in excess of potential market clearing rates.[53]

As long as the reins of power over the money supply remained in or near the hands of the government, Mises was convinced that the temptation for its use and abuse in the pursuit of short-run, political objectives was inevitable. Only the removal of the government's hand from the crank of the printing press could eliminate the historical pattern of booms and busts, inflations and depressions, induced misdirections of labor and capital with the resulting squandering of scarce resources, and general monetary debauchery.

But besides political economic grounds, Mises believed there were theoretical reasons for doubting the ability of a monetary authority to succeed in neutralizing money's impact on the real economy, reasons that separated him from most of the other Austrian economists of the interwar era. The implicit assumption among those Austrians who were attracted to the theoretical possibility of a neutral money policy was that one could disentangle those influences on the structure of relative prices that were due solely to real causes in the economy from those having their origin purely from the side of money. Their hesitations centered around the practical ability to undertake such a policy with the existing state of knowledge and institutional arrangements. The problems, as we saw, concerned the construction of the appropriate price indexes and the difficulty of directing the monetary changes to those points in the economy at which changes in the quantity of money in circulation were called for.

The heart of Mises' disagreement with the arguments for a neutral money was that it appeared to him as a will-o'-the-wisp just as illusive as the search for a "stable" money. It implicitly viewed money as an element *in* the economic system yet somehow *apart* and *separable* from it. In the 1920s Mises used much ink in arguing against those who at the time were advocating a policy of price level stabilization. He saw them as drawing a dichotomy between money and the real economy that was fundamentally flawed. On the one side was the real sector driven by and kept in order through a system of relative prices. On the other side was the quantity of money and the velocity at which that money turned over in facilitating the exchanges of the real sector. Changes in the supply of money or in its rate of turnover could influence the "level" of prices, but except during transition periods following a change in money or its velocity, the real economy was independent of the monetary lubricant that kept the parts in motion. Stabilization of the price level, it was claimed, would assure that disturbances from the money side would be neutralized. Any changes that then occurred would have their origin in and be limited to real changes on the sides of supply and demand.[54]

In contrast to this view of money's role in the economy, Mises insisted that money was not only *in* the economy, it was what *bound* the market process together into a single web of exchange. "Nothing can happen in the orbit of vendible goods without affecting the orbit of money," he argued, "and all that happens in the orbit of money affects the orbit of commodities."[55] In the nexus of exchange, money could be considered as the hub of a wheel holding together and connecting the spokes that represented the individual commodities of trade. Whatever occurred in the individual branches of industry was communicated to the rest of the system through the hub of money and any changes on the side of money were conveyed to the entire market through changes in the spectrum of individual exchange ratios between money and all of the goods of trade.[56] Everything that occurred on the side of the supply and demand for money, therefore, influenced and changed the relative prices of goods and everything that happened on the side of the individual supplies and demands for goods influenced and changed the general purchasing power of money.[57] The mirage of stable money dissolved away before the analyst's eyes as soon as money was seen as the one commodity always present on one side of every exchange, and every change in the relative prices between money and the individual goods against which it traded necessarily modified the value of money. As Mises starkly expressed it, the establishment of a stable money would require the freezing of all the relative prices among goods and between all the goods and money.[58]

The proposals for a neutral money were just as much a mirage, for here what was confused were conceptual tools of thought with the reality of the market process. When some of the other members of the Austrian school investigated the logical relationships between and the causal significance of various influences at work in the complex arena of goods and money, they utilized the basic devise of all mental experiments: ceteris paribus.[59] Various factors were held constant, some elements were assumed away and others were treated as having properties different from how they were actually found in the empirical world of experience. All such techniques were legitimate methods of theoretical analysis for the purpose of comprehending a world of complex phenomena in which all of these factors and elements were simultaneously at work and enmeshed in an intricate web of incessant change and adjustment.[60] But theoretical comprehension and empirical differentiation were worlds apart. It was precisely because of the difficulty or impossibility of the latter that the analyst had to make recourse to the former. To assume as differentiable in practice that which was only intelligible in theory was to confuse the domain of reality with the realm of ideas.

The fundamental flaw in the proposals for a neutral money was that a theoretical conception used for purposes of understanding the real price and production relationships in the economy—money (in substance, if not in form) treated as a *numeraire,* an element *in* the economy, but *not of it*—was considered of practical applicability. This confused an abstract concept of money with the reality of money in the *real* economy, a real economy in which money was inseparable from and integral to the ongoing market process. Money, in Mises' eyes, could be nothing but *nonneutral*, for it was the unique commodity that entered into one side of every act of exchange. Any change on the side of goods had its influence on the side of money by generating changes in incomes, demands, and therefore, the relative preferences for cash balance holdings; and every change in the individual demands for cash balances set out new ripples of change throughout the economy resulting in a new configuration of relative demands for goods.[61]

What, then, was the desirable end of monetary policy if neither stable nor neutral money were attainable goals? For Mises the answer was "sound" money. Sound money was a commodity money neither stable in value (because money's value, like all other goods' value, was a matter of relative prices) nor neutral in its effects on the economy (because of the pervasive presence of money in the nexus of exchange, which meant it was always a dynamic element for change). What sound money connoted was a monetary system fully integrated into and a part of the very market process which the use of money facilitated in growing, developing, and enhancing. What sound money was to be free of was the intervention of the political authorities, intervention that only succeeded, as Mises saw it, in producing economic disruption, social upheaval, deceptive taxation, and squandered capital—all through the false signals of manipulations of the money supply.

And why gold as the basis for a sound money system? Argued Mises:

> Because, as conditions are today and for the time that can be foreseen today, the gold standard alone makes the determination of money's purchasing power independent of the ambitions and machinations of governments, of dictators, of political parties, and of pressure groups. The gold standard alone is what the nineteenth-century freedom-loving leaders (who championed representative government, civil liberties and prosperity for all) called "sound money."[62]

The Gold Standard as Market Money

The gold standard, historically, was not seen by Mises as having been a monetary system fully integrated into the market economy. Through most of its modern history it had functioned in a twilight zone, partly in the market and partly under the influence of the state. The result was that it evolved in an extremely bastardized form, with government control increasing as the nineteenth century passed into the twentieth. Finally, with the outbreak of the First World War, the international gold standard—which had facilitated a hundred years of world economic growth and trade, and which had slowly integrated a set of national economies into a world economy—was first circumvented and then over-thrown in the flood of national paper monies that financed the war efforts of both sides in the War to End All War.[63]

During the years following both world wars, Mises participated in the discussions and debates on how a "sound money" gold standard could be established. Read in isolation his contributions on the subject could suggest that at various times his views on monetary reform changed significantly. When studied in conjunction with each other, however, the various arguments and proposals not only show themselves to be consistent with each other, but represent what Mises saw as, ideally, a step-by-step program for reform with the final goal being complete liberation of money from the political arena.

The first step on the road to monetary reform, Mises argued, had to be an immediate and complete end to all increases in the quantity of money by the central monetary authority.[64] Mises' rejection of what has come to be referred to as a "gradualist" policy of inflationary deceleration was argued for two reasons. First, he believed that only such a radical shift in policy could succeed in breaking inflationary expectations; second, there was no way to diminish the side effects of an inflation coming to an end. The argument frequently made today in defense of gradualism is that it would enable participants in the economy to adjust their prices and wage contracts in such a fashion that nominal values could more easily conform to the lower rates of monetary change, and, therefore, diminish any "real" effects on the economy that might arise from an end to inflation. However, the real effects from inflation in Mises' framework were not caused by a failure of the rates of change in prices and wages *in general* to conform to rates of monetary increase. Rather, the real effects of inflation were caused by money's differential and sequential effects on demands and prices during the inflationary process that gave a "wrong twist" to the distribution of labor and capital among alternative uses in the economy. Further inflation, even at a lower rate, offered no solution to the malinvestments already generated in the economy; all that continued monetary expansion could succeed in doing would be to delay the necessary corrections in the structure of production or, in fact, to distort the economic process further with even more adjustments called for at the end of the day.

Mises' own proposal for the next phase of monetary reform involved several stages. The *first stage* would involve three simultaneous steps:

First, a total prohibition on the issuance of any additional money and credit by the Central Monetary Authority;

Second, a 100% reserve requirement on all future deposits in the banking system;

> Third, complete freedom for all citizens to own, buy and sell gold, either domestically or in foreign markets, without any interference or intervention on the part of the government or the Federal Reserve.

The *second stage* would be undertaken after a period of time had elapsed:

> After the gold markets had settled down and a free market price had emerged between gold and dollars (free from any monetary manipulations on the part of the Monetary Authority) the government would declare a new parity at which dollars would be legally redeemed for gold.

The *third stage* would then involve the establishment of

> A Conversion Agency with the legal responsibility to convert dollars into gold (with the use of a gold fund "lent" from the Treasury interest free and for an indefinite period).

> The Treasury would be required afterwards to buy all dollars offered for sale by the Conversion Agency and extinguish, in cooperation with the Federal Reserve, all notes thus acquired.

> The Conversion Agency would also over time be required to mint and offer in exchange to dollar holders gold coins for small denomination notes (i.e., five, ten and twenty dollar bills).[65]

Mises' proposal for the establishment of a new parity rather than a reestablishment of a previous one followed from his analysis of the influence of money on the economy. Legal redemption at an older parity would require a contraction in the money supply until, in theory, all outstanding dollars could be exchanged for gold. However, just as a monetary expansion was nonneutral in its effects, so too was a monetary contraction. Employment, output, and the direction of production would all be adversely affected for as long as the contraction continued and had not completely worked its influence through the economy, with a fall in prices and wages.[66] In response to the argument that a monetary contraction following a monetary expansion merely compensated and corrected for the distortions caused during the inflation, Mises replied: "If a man has been hurt by being run over by an automobile, it is no remedy to let the car go back over him in the opposite direction."[67]

With the implementation of these reforms, the monetary system would have moved close to what Mises considered the positive aspects of the Currency School program as expressed in Peel's Bank Act of 1844.[68] While establishment of this much of a reform program would be considered a major step toward sound money, it was not the final step in Mises' mind. Total and complete removal of state control, influence, and power over the supply of money could be established and guaranteed only through the demise of central banking, *in any form*, and its replacement with a system of free banking.[69]

What inhibitions would exist under free banking to prevent the same type of monetary consequences as under central banking? To Mises the answer was clear: the forces of the market. Any bank that attempted to expand its note and credit issues in excess of rather conservative bounds would suffer the consequences of the reflux mechanism. In other words the principles that the classical economists had so lucidly explained under the heading of the specie-flow mechanism in trade between nations would operate in the same manner between competing, private banks doing business in the same political territory. A bank that expanded its note issue in excess of the demand to hold on the part of its clients would have those notes returned to it through the clearinghouse as those notes were presented for redemption by other banks on behalf of their clients. If the first bank's liabilities exceeded its possession of the note liabilities of the other banks, it would experience a reserve drain that would require a note contraction on its part to assure its solvency. Thus, the market process contained its own system of checks and balances to limit the expansion of money-substitutes on the basis of gold reserves.

And what determined the availability of gold? The profitability of gold production as determined, on the one hand, by gold's purchasing power as money and its price for industrial uses and, on the other hand, the costs of mining as reflected in the relative market values of factors of production in alternative uses. Freed from the discretion of political authority, money, like every other commodity in the circle of trade, would be under the sway of supply and demand. Money would now be fully integrated into the market process and totally subject, in the final analysis, to the preferences of consumers as demonstrated in voluntary acts of exchange.[70]

While the establishment of a system of sound money was considered a prerequisite by Mises for the operation of a free market, it was impossible to establish such a monetary system in isolation of other trends in the society and in the social fabric. The conquest of money by the state was indicative of an ideological conquest in society that saw prosperity through planning, equality through egalitarianism, freedom through force, and autonomy through autarky. A free money could only prevail, ultimately, in a free society. As Mises clearly expressed it at the height of the Great German Inflation:

> The belief that a sound monetary system can once again be attained without making substantial changes in economic policy is a serious

error. What is needed first and foremost is to renounce all inflationist fallacies. This renunciation cannot last, however, if it is not firmly grounded on a full and complete divorce of ideology from all imperialist, militarist, protectionist, statist, and socialist ideas.[71]

That is a task that falls upon all of us who desire to take up the Austrian heritage as exemplified in the writings of Ludwig von Mises.

Notes

1. Oskar Morgenstern, *The Limits of Economics* [1934] (London: William Hodge, 1937), p. 155. The English title is deceptive; the original German, *Die Grenzen der Wirtschaftspolitik*, more correctly captures the purpose of the book.
2. Cf. Alan R. Sweezy, "The Interpretation of Subjectivist Value Theory in the Writings of the Austrian Economists" *Review of Economic Studies*, 1 (1933–34):176: "In spite of a common tradition and far-reaching agreement on many points, the present group harbours deep-rooted differences of opinion in its midst."
3. Cf. Ludwig M. Lachmann, "The Significance of the Austrian School of Economics in the History of Ideas" [1966] in *Capital, Expectations and the Market Process* (Kansas City, Mo.: Sheed, Andrews, and McMeel, 1977), pp. 55–62.
4. Cf. F.A. Hayek, "The Transmission of the Ideals of Economic Freedom" [1951] in *Studies in Philosophy, Politics and Economics* (Chicago: University of Chicago Press, 1967), pp. 197–98; also, Hayek, "Appendix I: Tribute to Ludwig von Mises" [1956] in Margit von Mises, *My Years with Ludwig von Mises* (New Rochelle, N.Y.: Arlington House, 1976), pp. 189–90.
5. Carl Menger, "Geld" [1909] reprinted in *Grundsätze der Volkswirtschaftslehre* (Vienna: Holder-Pichler-Tempsky A.G., Zweite Auflage, 1923), pp. 325–31. This, of course, was consistent with Menger's general doubts about the construction and use of economic aggregates and his emphasis on always relating them back to the purposes of the individual agents whose actions brought them into existence; cf. his criticisms of the concept of "national wealth" in Carl Menger, *Principles of Economics* [1871] (New York: New York University Press [1950], reprinted 1981), pp. 111–13. On Menger's cash balance approach, see Arthur W. Marget, *The Theory of Prices*, vol. 1 [1938] (New York: Augustus M. Kelley, 1966), p. 418.
6. Eugen von Böhm-Bawerk, *Capital and Interest*, vol. 2, *The Positive Theory of Capital*, (South Holland, Ill.: Libertarian Press, 1959), pp. 77–118; also, cf. Ludwig M. Lachmann, "Böhm-Bawerk und die Kapitalstruktur," *Zeitschrift für Nationalökonomie* (August 1959): 235–45.
7. Knut Wicksell, *Interest and Prices* [1898] (New York: Augustus M. Kelley [1936], reprinted 1965), pp. 81–101.
8. The exact meaning of the term "natural rate" in Wicksell is not unambiguous; Marget, *The Theory of Prices*, vol. 1, pp. 201–4, was able to distinguish at least eight different senses of the natural rate in Wicksell's writings. The four most common ones were, the natural rate as (1) the anticipated rate of profit; (2) the rate at which savings equals investment; (3) the rate at which real capital

would be lent without the intermediation of money, that is, *in natura*; (4) the rate at which the price level remained stable. The first, the natural rate as the anticipated rate of profit seems to be the meaning Wicksell has in mind in the chapter titled "The Rate of Interest as Regulator of Commodity Prices," referred to in the preceding note.

9. This skewing effect of changes in the rate of interest on production decisions was later emphasized by Fritz Machlup in "The Rate of Interest as Cost Factor and as Capitalization Factor," *American Economic Review* (September 1935): 459–65; see also his earlier article, "The Liquidity of Short-term Capital," *Economica* (August 1932): 271–84.

10. Ludwig von Mises, *The Theory of Money and Credit* [1924] (Indianapolis: Liberty Classics [1952], reprinted 1981).

11. Ludwig von Mises, "Monetary Stabilization and Cyclical Policy" [1928] in *On the Manipulation of Money and Credit* (Dobbs Ferry, N.Y.: Free Market Books, 1978), pp. 57–171.

12. Carl Menger, *Principles of Economics*, pp. 257–71; *Problems of Economics and Sociology* [1883] (Urbana: University of Illinois Press, 1963), pp. 152–55; and "On the Origin of Money," *Economic Journal* (June 1892): 239–55.

13. An early criticism of marginal utility theory was that it claimed to explain the emergence of prices on the basis of the marginal evaluation of goods, but, the critics said, for a marginal evaluation of goods to occur, it was first necessary for there to exist ratios of exchange at which commodities could be traded and toward which evaluations could be directed; hence, the marginal utility theorists were accused of having to assume the existence of the very thing (prices) the theory was meant to explain, thus moving in a logical circle. On how the Austrians proposed to escape from the circle through the introduction of *expectations* and the distinction between *expected* prices and *realized* prices, see, Böhm-Bawerk, *Capital and Interest* vol. 2, pp. 240–43; Leo Schönfeld-Illy, *Das Gesetz des Grenznutzen* (Vienna: 1948), pp. 183–238; and Israel M. Kirzner, *Market Theory and the Price System* (Princeton, N.J.: D. Van Nostrand, 1963), pp. 105–41.

Similar criticisms were leveled against the application of marginal utility theory to explain the value of money. Mises argued that it was true that the evaluation of the marginal utility of money was dependent upon the preexistence of the monetary unit having a specific purchasing power. Since money was directly serviceable neither for consumption nor for production but, rather, acquired its utility as a good on the basis that it could be held in the form of cash balances to facilitate future acts of exchange, any present demand for the money good presupposed it having an existing purchasing power. But logically no circular reasoning was involved, Mises argued. Money's present purchasing power could be "regressed" back to that point at which the money good was used for the first time as a medium of exchange, before which the commodity's exchange value would have been based purely upon its utility as a consumption and/or production good; Mises, *The Theory of Money and Credit*, pp. 129–46; also, Mises, *Human Action, A Treatise on Economics* 3rd ed. (Chicago: Henry Regnery, 1966), pp. 408–16.

14. Like Menger, Mises rejected the analytical usefulness of the concept of the velocity of circulation of money. He argued that both the velocity concept

and the equation of exchange, of which the concept was a component, were methodologically inappropriate as theoretical devices in the service of economic reasoning, both being carryovers of an earlier methodological holism; Mises, "The Position of Money among Economic Goods" [originally published in German in *Die Wirtschaftstheorie der Gegenwart*, vol. 2, edited by Hans Mayer, Frank A. Fetter, and Richard Reisch (Vienna: Julius Springer, 1932) to be included in a volume of Mises' essays edited by me]:

> The attempts to solve the problem of the value of money with reference to the economy as a whole, rather than through market factors, culminated in a tautological equation without any epistemological value. Only a theory which shows how subjective value judgments of buyers and sellers are influenced by changes in the different elements of the equation of exchange can legitimately be called a theory of the value of money.
>
> Buyers and sellers on the market never concern themselves with the elements in the equation of exchange of which two—velocity of circulation and the price level—do not even exist before market parties act and the other two—the quantity of money (in the economy as a whole) and the sum of transactions—could not possibly be known to the parties in the market. The importance which the various actors in the market attach, on the one hand, to the maintenance of a cash balance of a certain magnitude and, on the other hand, to the ownership of the various goods in question determines the formation of the exchange relationships between money and goods.

Cf. also, *Human Action*, pp. 399–400.

15. Mises, *The Theory of Money and Credit*, pp. 160–68 and 237–43; *Nation, State and Economy* [1919] (New York: New York University Press, 1983), pp. 155–58; "Monetary Stabilization and Cyclical Policy," pp. 95–96; *Human Action*, pp. 412–16; and "The Non-Neutrality of Money" an unpublished paper delivered at the Ecole Pratique des Hautes Etudes in Paris (May 1939) and at the Political Economy Club in New York (November 1940) to be included in a volume of essays by Mises edited by me.

16. The different meanings of the "real effects" of monetary expansion or contraction in the writings of quantity theorists has not always been explicitly brought out. I hope to clarify the distinctions in a future paper, "Alternative Theories of the Non-Neutrality of Money: Fisher and Mises."

17. In some places Mises uses the "natural rate" to signify that rate at which intertemporal loans would be made *in natura*, see, *The Theory of Money and Credit*, pp. 393–94; and "Monetary Stabilization and Cyclical Policy," p. 122. In other places the "natural rate" is defined as the loan market rate at which investment would be equal to savings, see *The Theory of Money and Credit*, pp. 399–400; and "Monetary Stabilization and Cyclical Policy," p. 124; for Mises' more sophisticated explanation of the meaning of the equilibrium loan market rate(s)—one that incorporates time preference, the risk factor in the evaluation of individual loans and any "premiums" for changes anticipated in the purchasing power of money—see *Human Action*, pp. 538–48.

18. Mises' expositions of his theory of the trade cycle can be found in *The Theory of Money and Credit*, pp. 396–404; "Monetary Stabilization and Cyclical Policy," pp. 118–30; and *Human Action*, pp. 550–75.

19. In *The Theory of Money and Credit*, pp. 399–401, Mises refers to the effects of credit expansion as involving a "lengthening of the average period of production." In *Human Action*, pp. 556–58, the questionable Böhm-Bawerkian terminology is left behind and the focus is rather on the fact that the lowered money rate of interest and additional credit set off the undertaking of investment activities of varying types, shapes, and forms (not just a "lengthening") that will be found to be unsustainable in view of the savings available to maintain the capital structure of the economy.

20. On the effect of unemployed resources in the initial stages of the upturn, see Mises, "Monetary Stabilization and Cyclical Policy," p. 125; and *Human Action*, pp. 578–80.

21. Ludwig von Mises, "Inconvertible Capital" [1931] in *Epistemological Problems of Economics* [1933] (New York: New York University Press [1960], reprinted 1981), pp. 225–31.

22. Mises argued that the changes in relative income shares during the monetary expansion could, in theory, bring about a permanent change in the rate of interest if the modifications in wealth positions among social groups was from those with higher time preference to those with lower time preference. But whether this occurred would depend upon the circumstances of the historical case, no a priori argument on the matter could be made. On the possibility of "forced saving," see *The Theory of Money and Credit*, pp. 238–39, and "Monetary Stabilization and Cyclical Policy," pp. 121 and 126–27. For an account of the development of the "forced saving" concept in the nineteenth century, see, Friedrich A. Hayek, *Prices and Production* (New York: Augustus M. Kelley [1935], reprinted 1967), pp. 101–4; and Hayek, "A Note on the Development of the Doctrine of 'Forced Saving'" [1932], reprinted in *Profits, Interest, and Investment* [1939] (New York: Augustus M. Kelley, 1969), pp. 183–97.

23. It is perhaps of interest to note that C. Bresciani-Turroni, in a review of Hayek's *Monetary Theory and the Trade Cycle* (*Economica* (August, 1934): p. 347), believed that the Austrian theory was very instructive in explaining the course of the Great German Inflation of the early 1920s:

The changes in the structure of production, brought about by inflation, and later by currency stabilization, were most apparent in Germany. During the inflation period the substantial fall in real wages, which meant a "forced saving" on a large scale, allowed the productive resources of the country to be deflected from the production of consumer goods to that of fixed capital. This continued as long as the new issues of paper money exerted a pressure upon real wages. But the situation changed when the value of money was stabilized. Then an adjustment of real wages began, which showed the insufficiency of the "fund for the maintenance of labor." The demand for consumers' goods increased, that of producers' goods on the whole declined, and the prices of the latter diminished relatively to those of the former. This resulted in a redistribution of productive resources. A shift to the production of consumers' goods was distinctively observed in 1924. The so-called "stabilization crisis" with its most striking feature, the "scarcity of capital," was nothing else than a readjustment of the whole structure of production, which had been distorted during the inflation period.

Cf. Bresciani-Turroni's *The Economics of Inflation* [1931] (New York: Augustus M. Kelley [1937], reprinted 1968), pp. 183–223 and 359–97.

24. Friedrich A. Von Hayek, *Monetary Theory and the Trade Cycle* [1929] (New York: Augustus M. Kelley [1933], reprinted 1966); *Prices and Production* [1st ed., 1931] (New York: Augustus M. Kelley [2nd revised ed. 1935], reprinted 1967); *Profits, Interest and Investment* (New York: Augustus M. Kelley [1939], reprinted 1969).

25. Lionel Robbins, "Consumption and the Trade Cycle," *Economica* (November 1932), pp. 413–30; *the Great Depression* (New York: Macmillan, 1934); "The Twofold Roots of The Great Depression: Inflationism and Interventionism," in *The Burden of Plenty*, edited by Graham Hutton (London: George Allen and Unwin, 1935).

26. Gottfried Haberler, "Money and the Business Cycle" [1932] reprinted in *The Austrian Theory of the Trade Cycle and Other Essays*, by Ludwig von Mises, Gottfried Haberler, Murray Rothbard, and Friedrich A. Hayek (Washington, D.C.: The Ludwig von Mises Institute [1978], reprinted 1983), pp. 7–20.

27. Fritz Machlup, *The Stock Market, Credit and Capital Formation* [1931] (London: William Hodge, revised ed. 1940); *Fuhrer durch die Krisenpolitik* (Vienna: Julius Springer, 1934); "Can We Control the Boom?" A Conference at the University of Minnesota, May 11, 1937, *The Day and Hour Series*, no. 20 (The University of Minnesota Press, October 1937), pp. 11–18.

28. Erich Schiff, *Kapitalbildung und Kapitalaufzehrung im Konjunkturlauf* (Vienna: Julius Springer, 1933).

29. Richard von Strigl, *Kapital und Produktion* [1934] (Munich and Vienna: Philosophia Verlag, 1982); "Der Wicksellsche Prozess," *Weltwirtschaftliches Archiv*, bd. 60 (1942): 443–64.

30. Frederic Benham, *British Monetary Policy* (London: P.S. King and Son, 1932).

31. H.F. Fraser, *Great Britain and the Gold Standard* (London: Macmillan, 1933).

32. T.E. Gregory, *Gold, Unemployment and Capitalism* (London: P.S. King and Son, 1933), p. xiii: "Whilst I am by no means an adherent of the terminology or even of some of the tenets of the Viennese School, I do believe that they are right in thinking that in the course of upward movement of the trade cycle profound modifications in the structure of production take place and that monetary policy or theory cannot be negligent of this aspect in putting forward remedial measures."

33. M.A. Abrams, *Money and a Changing Civilization* (London: John Lane, The Bodley Head, 1934).

34. E.F.M. Durbin, *Purchasing Power and Trade Depression* (London: Jonathan Cape, 1934); *The Problem of Credit Policy* (London: Chapman and Hall, 1935); "Money and Prices," in *What Everybody Wants to Know about Money*, edited by G.D.H. Cole (New York: Alfred A. Knopf, 1933), pp. 253–79.

35. H.T.N. Gaitskell, "Four Monetary Heretics," in Cole, ed., *What Everybody Wants to Know about Money*, pp. 280–335.

36. C.A. Phillips, T.F. McManus, and R.W. Nelson, *Banking and the Business Cycle* [1937] (New York: Arno Press and The New York Times, 1972).

37. Albert L. Meyers, *Elements of Modern Economics* (New York: Prentice-Hall, 1937), pp. 278–93 and 336–49.

38. Robbins, *The Great Depression*, pp. 164–72.

39. See note 8 supra.

40. Members of the "Stockholm School," also working in the Wicksellian tradition, came to similar conclusions; see Erik Lindahl, "The Rate of Interest and the Price Level" [1930] in *Studies in the Theory of Money and Capital* [1939] (New York: Augustus M. Kelley, 1970), pp. 139–268; Gunnar Myrdal, *Monetary Equilibrium* [1933] (New York: Augustus M. Kelley, 1965).

41. Hayek, *Monetary Theory and the Trade Cycle*, pp. 113–14; *Prices and Production*, pp. 23–28.

42. Hayek, *Prices and Production*, pp. 105–28; and *Monetary Nationalism and International Stability* [1937] (New York: Augustus M. Kelley, 1971) pp. 73–94. As late as 1960, Hayek still believed in the necessity for a government monopoly over the money supply; see *The Constitution of Liberty* (Chicago: University of Chicago Press, 1960), pp. 324–339. Only in *Choice in Currency* [1976], reprinted in *New Studies in Philosophy, Politics, Economics and the History of Ideas* (Chicago: University of Chicago Press, 1978), pp. 218–231, and more fully in *Denationalization of Money* (London: Institute of Economic Affairs [1976], revised ed., 1978) did Hayek conclude that monetary stability could only be approached through a divorce of money from state control, through a system of competitive currencies issued by private banks; however, his proposal for private moneys was not one based on the gold standard, but rather on fiat currencies whose values would be stabilized by the banks on the basis of an index of commodity prices. For a critical analysis of Hayek's proposal, see Richard Ebeling, "Decontrolling Money," *Libertarian Review* (March-April 1977). Hayek's suggestion in *Choice in Currency* that a way to curb governmental inflationary policies was to eliminate legal tender laws and allow citizens of each country to domestically use any national currency that found preferable was, in fact (though Hayek doesn't mention it), proposed much earlier by Richard Strigl, "Gibt es eine Sicherung gegen Inflation?" *Mitteilungen des Verbandes osterreichischer Banken und Bankiers* (1932) N. 15/6.

43. Gottfried Haberler, *The Different Meanings Attached to the Term "Fluctuations in the Purchasing Power of Gold" and the Best Instrument or Instruments for Measuring Such Fluctuations.* Official No. F/Gold/74 (Geneva: League of Nations, March 9, 1931).

44. Gottfried Haberler, *The Theory of International Trade* [1933] (London: William Hodges, 1936) p. 47.

45. Fritz Machlup, *The Stock Market, Credit and Capital Formation*, pp. 174–201; also cf. Machlup, "Inflation and Decreasing Costs of Production," in *Economics of Inflation*, edited by H. Parker Willis and John M. Chapman (New York: Columbia University Press, 1935), pp. 280–87.

46. Alexander Mahr, *Monetary Stability, and How to Achieve It*, Public Policy Pamphlets, no. 9 (Chicago: University of Chicago Press, 1933); and Mahr,

"Technological Progress and Monetary Policy" in *Guest Lectures in Economics, Twenty Lectures Delivered in English at Professor G.U. Papi's Seminar, Institute of Economics and Public Finance, Faculty of Law, University of Rome, 1956–1961*, edited by Elizabeth Henderson and Luigi Spaventa (Milan: Dott. A. Giuffre, 1962), pp. 144–53.

47. Mises, "Monetary Stabilization and Cyclical Policy," p. 78; *The Theory of Money and Credit*, p. 416; *Human Action*, p. 474.

48. Mises, *Human Action*, p. 781.

49. Mises, *The Theory of Money and Credit*, pp. 222–23; *Nation, State and Economy*, pp. 151–65; "Stabilization of the Monetary Unit—from the Viewpoint of Theory" [1923] in *On the Manipulation of Money and Credit*, pp. 36–38.

50. Mises, *Human Action*, p. 403; "The Gold Problem," in *Planning for Freedom*, 4th ed. (South Holland, Ill.: Libertarian Press, 1980), pp. 187–90.

51. Mises, "Lord Keynes and Say's Law," in *Planning for Freedom*, pp. 64–71.

52. Mises, "The Causes of the Economic Crisis: An Address," 1931 in *On the Manipulation of Money and Credit*, pp. 199–200.
ian Perspective

53. Mises, "Gold versus Paper," *The Freeman* (July 13, 1953) pp. 744–46; "Full Employment and Monetary Policy," *National Review* (June 22, 1957); 589–91.

54. Mises, *The Theory of Money and Credit*, pp. 236–38 and 399–406; "Monetary Stabilization and Cyclical Policy," pp. 90–98; and *The Suitability of Methods of Ascertaining Changes in Purchasing Power for the Guidance of International Currency and Banking Policy*, Official No. F/Gold/51 (Geneva: League of Nations, October 10, 1930), the latter a previously unpublished monograph written for the League of Nations, to be included in a volume of essays by Mises edited by me.

55. Mises, *Human Action*, p. 418.

56. Mises followed some of the classical economists (cf. Jacob Viner, *Studies in the Theory of International Trade* [1937] [New York: Augustus M. Kelley, 1965], pp. 311–14) in defining the purchasing power of money as the spectrum of individual exchange ratios between money and the goods against which it traded, see *The Theory of Money and Credit*, p. 188; *Human Action*, p. 402. Also cf. Murray N. Rothbard, *Man. Economy and State*, vol. 1 [1962] (Los Angeles: Nash, 1970), p. 205.

57. The dynamics of money's influence on the structure of relative prices as well as the ever changing character of supply and demand in general resulted in Mises declaring all attempts to scientifically measure changes in the purchasing power of money as insoluble. All the methods and techniques for the construction of index numbers were considered both static in quality and arbitrary in nature; cf. *The Theory of Money and Credit*, pp. 187–94; "Monetary Stabilization and Cyclical Policy," pp. 83–89; *The Suitability of Methods of Ascertaining Changes in Purchasing Power for the Guidance of International Currency and Banking Policy*; *Human Action*, pp. 220–23. A similar conclusion had been reached by the well-known Dutch economist, N.G. Pierson in the late nineteenth century, "Further Considerations on Index Numbers," *Economic Journal* (March 1896):131: "the only possible conclusion seems to be that all attempts to calculate and represent average movements of prices, either by index numbers or otherwise ought to be abandoned." On the problems with index numbers as a

measure for changes in purchasing power, see the excellent and entertaining book by Bassett Jones, *Horses and Apples, A Study in Index Numbers* (New York: John Day, 1934); also, Michael A. Heilperin, *International Monetary Economics* (London: Longmans, Green, 1939), the appendix on "Note on the Use of Statistical Constructions," pp. 259–70; and John W. Robbins, *The Case Against Indexation*, Monetary Tract no. 16 (Greenwich, Conn.: Committee for Monetary Research and Education, July 1976); for a statistician's objections, M.J. Moroney, *Facts from Figures* (London: Penguin Books, 1953), pp. 48–55.

It is perhaps of interest to note that on the question of measuring changes in the purchasing power of money and the assumptions that money confronts a selection of goods whose relative prices among one another are either constant or uninfluenced from the side of money, Mises and Keynes held similar views; cf. John Maynard Keynes, *A Treatise on Money*, vol. 1 (New York: Harcourt Brace, 1930), pp. 79–88; and on money's influence on the structure of relative prices, the very "Austrian"-type passages on pp. 92–94.

58. Mises, "Monetary Stabilization and Cyclical Policy," p. 84; see the similar conclusion by Menger, "Geld," p. 299; and on Menger's views on the insolubility of stabilizing the value of money, see Charles Rist, *History of Monetary and Credit Theory* [1938] (New York: Augustus M. Kelley [1940], reprinted 1966), pp. 372–73.

59. Mises, "Monetary Stabilization and Cyclical Policy," pp. 85–86.

60. Mises, *Human Action*, pp. 236–37, on the use of imaginary constructions.

61. Mises, "The Non-Neutrality of Money."

62. Mises, "The Gold Problem," p. 185.

63. Mises, *The Theory of Money and Credit*, pp. 368–90; *Human Action*, pp. 471–76.

64. Mises, "Stabilization of the Monetary Unit—from the Viewpoint of Theory," p. 17; *The Theory of Money and Credit*, p. 448.

65. Mises, *The Theory of Money and Credit*, pp. 448–52.

66. Mises, *The Theory of Money and Credit*, pp. 452–56.

67. Mises, "The Non-Neutrality of Money."

68. Mises, "Monetary Stabilization and Cyclical Policy," p. 168.

69. Mises, *Human Action*, p. 443.

70. Mises, *The Theory of Money and Credit*, pp. 395–99; "Monetary Stabilization and Cyclical Policy," pp. 138–40; *Human Action*, pp. 434–48.

71. Mises, "Stabilization of the Monetary Unit—from the Viewpoint of Theory," p. 49.

4
The Costs of a Gold Standard

Roger W. Garrison

T he term *gold standard,* whether used in a historical or a theoretical context, can mean many different things. And for each meaning of this term, a reference to the costs of a gold standard will not be unambiguous. Yet it is commonly believed, by economists and laypersons alike, that cost considerations eliminate gold as a viable medium of exchange in modern-day economies.

The purpose of this chapter is to examine the arguments against the gold standard which are based on considerations of costs. The benefits of a gold standard are identified in order to put the discussion of costs into proper perspective, then two conflicting views of the gold standard and of the resources devoted to maintaining it are compared. After a discussion of actual estimates of the resource costs of gold, the more broadly conceived concept of *opportunity costs* is used to argue the irrelevance of *resource costs* to the comparison of alternative monetary institutions. Finally, the assumed equivalence of monetary stability and price-level stability is called into question. This assumption, which underlies many of the cost estimates, has clouded some fundamental issues in ways that have prejudiced both monetary theorists and policymakers against the gold standard.

The Gold Standard: Costs and Benefits

Any discussion of the costs of a gold standard and of the controversy that surrounds this issue is, by its very nature, a one-sided discussion. The comparison of alternative standards on the basis of costs will not be meaningful unless the corresponding benefits are brought into view. Spelling out the particular type of gold standard being discussed and identifying its benefits—in comparison to a paper standard—puts the

I would like to acknowledge the helpful comments and criticisms offered by Don Bellante, Don Boudreaux, and Leland B. Yeager of Auburn University and Gerald P. O'Driscoll, Jr., of the Federal Reserve Bank of Dallas.

cost comparisons into proper perspective and goes a long way toward justifying the costs.

The term *gold standard* in the present chapter is used to denote the outcome of a market process. Using the term in this way serves to consolidate at least three propositions—based on both economic theory and historical insight—about the nature of markets and about the nature of money. (1) Left to its own devices, a market economy will give rise to a medium of exchange.[1] (2) The commodity that emerges as the medium of exchange will be one that possesses a certain set of characteristics.[2] (3) This set of characteristics has its clearest and most pronounced manifestation in gold.[3] So conceived, the gold standard, at least in its purest form, neither requires nor permits the state to exercise control over the money supply. And, as argued below in this chapter, the absence of centralized, discretionary monetary control constitutes the primary benefit of the gold standard.

The perception by the layperson that the costs of a gold standard are too high is not difficult to understand. Under a gold standard suppliers of goods or of labor services exchange their supplies for gold (or for banknotes redeemable in gold) not because the gold standard is seen as having great merit, but because gold is the customarily accepted medium of exchange. To each market participant gold *per se* has no particular benefits, although the custom of accepting some specific thing does. When consciously pondering the nature of money, the layperson is likely to see the custom in a different context and to see the value that others attach to gold—or that the market attaches to gold—as irrational, as being based on superstition or mythology. Gold in the layperson's view is a "barbarous relic" (to use Maynard Keynes's phrase). Yet individuals in modern economies continue to devote resources to securing this shiny yellow metal. Could not some other custom have the same benefits without having such high costs?

Market-oriented economists adopt a third view of the gold standard, one that differs from the views of both the market participant and the layperson pondering the gold question. The economists see the difficulties —and costs—of replacing an evolved custom with a designed system. The differences among such economists stem from the differing estimates of the nature and magnitude of these difficulties.

Economists who oppose the gold standard may recognize what has to be achieved in order to make a centrally controlled paper standard superior to a decentralized gold standard. Milton Friedman poses the key question, "[H]ow ... can we establish a monetary system that is stable, free from irresponsible tinkering, and incapable of being used as a source of power to threaten economic and political freedom?"[4] How, in other words, can we design a system that we cannot tinker with? While Friedman goes on to suggest how such a system might be designed, economists who support the gold standard argue that this objective is self-contradictory and operationally impossible. Any monetary institution that is designed and implemented by a central authority can be abused by that central authority.

The proponents of gold are not suggesting that irresponsible tinkering is inevitable, whatever the nature of the monetary system; they are instead making the sharp distinction between a designed institution and an evolved institution. A monetary institution that has been consciously designed is much more subject to tinkering than one that simply emerged as a consequence of market processes. F.A. Hayek points to the positivist slogan that "what man has made he can also alter to suit his desires."[5] The positivists were correct so long as they were referring to consciously and deliberately designed institutions such as a paper standard. Of course, it is government officials (not "man") who design the paper standard, and it is government officials who can (and do) tinker with it. Hayek goes on to point out the limits of the positivists' view. The slogan is a "complete *non-sequitur* if 'made' is understood to include what has arisen from man's actions without his design."[6]

A gold standard—one that has emerged as a consequence of market processes—cannot easily be altered to suit the state's purposes. It would be an overstatement (and a matter of historical inaccuracy) to claim that the state cannot in the long run interfere with the operation of the gold standard. What is true (both theoretically and historically) is that the state can supplant a spontaneously evolved monetary system with a centrally controlled system only after a prolonged struggle in which it must slowly and gradually overcome (through propaganda and the use of coercion) the market's reluctance to abandon gold. It is the gold standard's substantial immunity from state manipulation and tinkering, and not the associated superstition and mythology, that recommends gold as a monetary standard. In the words of Ludwig von Mises, "The advantage of the gold standard ... is due solely to the fact that, if once generally adopted in a definite form, and adhered to, it is no longer subject to specific political interference."[7] In the judgment of the proponents of the gold standard, the benefits of gold, immunity from state intervention and the resulting monetary stability, outweigh the resource costs of gold and any other costs that might be associated with the gold standard—by a comfortable margin.

The Resources Devoted to Gold: Too Few and Too Many

Discussions of the gold standard typically gravitate toward a consideration of the amount of resources used up in the maintenance of it. Well-recognized market processes devote a certain amount of resources to the gold-mining industry, sometimes more resources, sometimes fewer, depending upon market conditions in the rest of the economy. Changing market conditions have both price effects and quantity effects that come into play. Consider, for instance, an increase in the demand for money brought about by a desire on the part of market participants for greater liquidity. This demand shift puts downward pressure on prices. Because the actual adjustment in prices is not immediate, the increased monetary demand will have a temporary effect on quantities as well. Excess supplies of goods and of resources—both labor and capital—will develop. In general, the more rapidly the prices adjust, the less pronounced the temporary adjustment in quantities, and conversely, the more slowly they adjust, the more pronounced the adjustment in quantities.

The adjustment process is facilitated in part by changing market conditions in the gold-mining industry and in supporting industries. In these markets, movements in prices and quantities are opposite in direction to the movements in markets for goods that exchange against money. Downward movements of prices in general mean an increased value of the monetary commodity; excess supplies of labor and capital mean an increased availability of resources for mining gold. Both the price and the quantity effects stimulate the production of the monetary commodity and in the process relieve the pressure that gave rise to the stimulation. The final result is that the increased demand for money is accommodated in part by an actual decline in prices and in part by an increased quantity of the monetary commodity. The relative size of the two accommodating factors depends upon the supply conditions in the gold-mining industry.

Much of the dissatisfaction with the gold standard stems from dissatisfaction with the quantity of resources devoted to the extraction and processing of gold. Paradoxically, some opponents of gold believe that too few resources are involved for the gold standard to be viable, while other opponents believe that too many resources are devoted to the mining of gold. Not surprisingly, these opposing opponents of gold are reasoning in markedly different ways.

The first line of reasoning is based on the assumption that prices are extremely "sticky," and hence that all adjustments to changing market conditions are quantity adjustments. An increased demand for money means a decreased demand for goods. Since the goods cannot all be sold at existing prices, surpluses pile up, production is curtailed, and workers become unemployed. An economy-wide depression sets in. The only excess demand in the economy is for the monetary commodity. But because of the nature of gold—its relative scarcity—the gold-mining industry can absorb only a small fraction of the unemployment. The demand for money cannot be fully met at the existing level of prices. If the gold-mining industry absorbed the same amount of resources that were unemployed as a result of the increase in the demand for money, then the gold standard would perform admirably in this view and would constitute an automatic countercyclical device. Employment could shift from goods to gold or from gold to goods, but the level of employment would remain unchanged. Unfortunately, the gold-mining industry does not employ enough labor and capital resources to provide for such economic stability.[8] This line of reasoning has even caused one monetary reformer to advocate the abandonment of gold and the adoption of the common clay brick as a monetary standard.[9]

The other line of reasoning considers the alternative of a centrally directed system of paper money that can mimic the countercyclical effects of a clay-brick standard but without devoting any resources at all to the production of clay bricks or to the mining of gold. Each increase in the demand for money could be met with a costlessly produced increase in the quantity of money supplied. An economy whose transactions are facilitated by such a managed paper money would never experience an economy-wide downward pressure on prices that could result in resource idleness. Thus, the economy could devote all its resources to the production of real (nonmonetary) output. With this possibility in mind the allocation of any of the economy's resources to the production of gold is seen as wasteful and as constituting too many resources.[10]

Proponents of the gold standard should not feel called upon to argue in the context of either of these two lines of reasoning that the quantity of resources actually devoted to gold is just enough but not too much. Practically any quantity would at the same time be too little and too much, depending upon the opponent's particular point of view. Both viewpoints, however, can be called into question by an examination of the meaning and relevance of key concepts used by each. Particularly critical to the issue of the gold standard are the concepts of costs, resource costs, price stability, and monetary stability. These and related concepts provide a focus for the remainder of the present chapter.

The Costs of Gold and the Costs of a Constant Price Level

Estimates of the resource costs of gold depend critically upon the assumed rate of extraction. The actual rate of extraction, as indicated in the previous section, would be determined by market conditions. In an expanding economy with given supply conditions for gold, an increasing demand for money would cause additional resources to be committed to gold-mining operations. If competitive forces in the banking industry have given rise to the circulation of redeemable banknotes, the actual shift in the demand for gold caused by the expansion would be significantly reduced. The additional quantity of resources committed to gold would depend upon the elasticity of supply and the magnitude of the demand shift. Gold's relative inelasticity of supply would ensure that the dominant effect of the increase in the demand for gold, whatever its magnitude, would be a price effect rather than a quantity effect. That is, the value of gold would rise, or conversely, the prices of other goods would fall with respect to gold. There would be some increase in the quantity of gold supplied, but due to the price effect, this increase would be small in comparison with the increase in demand. The resource costs of extracting the additional gold would be correspondingly small.

Unfortunately, the most commonly cited estimates of the resource costs are based on the assumptions that there is no circulation of banknotes and that there is no price effect at all. Further, the supply of gold is assumed to be perfectly elastic.[11] Increases in the demand for money, under these assumptions, are met in full with increases in the quantity of gold supplied. The rate of gold extraction, in other words, is assumed to be sufficiently large to offset totally the downward movement of prices that would otherwise be necessary in an expanding economy. The fact that the supply of gold is actually *inelastic* is simply brushed aside. The resulting estimate of the resource costs, then, is not an estimate of the costs of a gold standard at all but rather an estimate of the costs of maintaining a constant price level by adopting an elastically supplied commodity money.

Not surprisingly, actual estimates that are based on these assumptions show that the costs of a commodity money are quite high. Neglecting changes in the velocity of money, Friedman calculated that for the first half of the twentieth century, the resource costs of a pure gold standard would have amounted to about 1.5 percent of national income, or about one-half of the annual growth rate of output. (Velocity considerations would increase these figures to 2 percent of national income and two-thirds of the annual growth rate.)[12] These particular estimates are three decades out of date, but the estimating procedure is in current use. Allan Meltzer cites the Friedman estimate and then updates the figures to reflect the current ratio of money to income. The new calculations indicate that the costs are down from 50 percent of the annual growth rate to something like 16 percent. But the cost of a gold standard in Meltzer's own judgment "remains high."[13]

The estimating procedure adopted by Friedman and more recently by Meltzer is flawed on both positive and normative grounds. The positive analysis makes use of the classical long-run perspective in which *all* supply curves are perfectly elastic. Friedman notes explicitly that his cost estimate is independent of which commodity is used as the monetary standard.[14] Perfect supply elasticity is a particularly inappropriate assumption when the gold standard is at issue. The supply of gold is inelastic in the short run because of the increasing marginal costs of extraction and inelastic in the long run because of the natural scarcity of this particular element. Friedman's and Meltzer's calculations fail to take into account these particular supply considerations which help to qualify gold as a monetary commodity. Indeed, they fail to make any distinction whatsoever between gold and all other commodities.

The normative judgment upon which their cost calculations are based is the judgment that the maintenance of a constant price level over time is an undisputed *desideratum* and the appropriate basis for evaluating alternative monetary arrangements. The significance of a constant price level in this regard is the focus of the penultimate section of the present chapter. The following two sections distinguish between two different cost concepts and question the use of resource costs as a criteria for choosing among alternative monetary institutions.

Costs, Resource Costs, and the Gold Standard

It was demonstrated earlier in this chapter that commonly cited estimates of the resource costs of gold are based on untenable assumptions about the supply conditions in the gold-mining industry and about the desired behavior of the price level. In this section the focus is on the relevance of any estimate of resource costs to the comparison of gold and paper standards. It is argued that the resource costs are doubly irrelevant in assessing the relative merits and the relative costs of the two alternative standards. The critical issues are likely to be overlooked if there is a failure to distinguish between (1) the resource costs of gold and (2) the costs of a gold standard. The two cost concepts are totally dissimilar despite the similarity in verbiage. This section deals with the costs of the gold and paper standards over and above the narrowly conceived resource costs; the following section puts the resource costs of gold into proper perspective.

So-called resource costs are an inadequate proxy for total costs or opportunity costs, unless the former term is defined in such a way as to make it synonymous with the latter two, in which case the modifier *resource* becomes redundant and misleading. The inadequacy is especially pronounced when the issue is the relative costs of alternative institutional arrangements.[15] A penal system that segregates convicted criminals from the rest of society may involve more resource costs than one that only slaps the criminals' wrists and turns them back into society. But it would be difficult to argue that the total costs, which would have to take into account the subsequent crimes perpetrated by convicted criminals, are greater for the former institutional arrangement than for the latter.

There is a similar difficulty in the argument that a gold standard costs more than a paper standard. Comparing the resource costs of gold to the resource costs of paper does not settle the issue. The true costs of the paper standard would have to take into account (1) the costs imposed on society by different political factions in their attempts to gain control of the printing press, (2) the costs imposed by special-interest groups in their attempts to persuade the controller of the printing press to misuse its authority (print more money) for the benefit of the special interests, (3) the costs in the form of inflation-induced misallocations of resources that occur throughout the economy as a result of the monetary authority succumbing to the political pressures of the special interests, and (4) the costs incurred by businesses in their attempts to predict what the monetary authority will do in the future and to hedge against likely, but uncertain, consequences of monetary irresponsibility. With these considerations in mind, it is not difficult to believe that a gold standard costs less than a paper standard. The judgment that a gold standard is the less costly reflects the wisdom in a simile attributed to Alan Greenspan: Allowing the state to create paper money is like putting a penny in the fuse box. The resource costs of the penny may be lower than the resource costs of the fuse, but the total costs, which take into account the likelihood of a destructive fire, are undoubtedly higher.

Some proponents of a paper standard base their counterarguments on their perception of the costs of a gold standard over and above the narrowly defined resource costs. But it is difficult to produce a laundry list of costs that will rival the list that was easily produced for the paper standard. The one cost most commonly cited stems from the fact that the supply of gold is *not* perfectly elastic, that gold production chronically falls short of real economic growth.[16] This circumstance requires that the price level be continually adjusted downward as the ratio of money to real output steadily declines. And the market process by which individual prices become so adjusted can be time-consuming and costly. Monetary disequilibrium, in effect, gets translated into disequilibrium in all markets throughout the economy.[17] Until equilibrium is eventually restored, the disequilibrium prices will result in the misdirection of some resources and the idleness of others. Under a paper standard, the monetary authority can eliminate the need to continually adjust prices by continually increasing the money supply to keep pace with the economy's real growth.

At one level of abstraction, the opponents of the gold standard have an appealing, if not compelling, argument. But when the analysis penetrates beneath the issue of the changing price *levels* associated with the gold and paper standards, the argument all but disappears. At least three considerations are relevant here.[18] First, individual prices in a market economy are changing all the time in response to changing market conditions. Some prices are increasing, some decreasing. If the supply of gold is not increasing as fast as real output, the pattern of individual price changes will be altered. Prices that are increasing will not increase quite so much; prices that are falling will have to fall a little further. Some prices that would have had to be increased a little will not have to be increased at all; some which would have remained unchanged will have to be slightly decreased. As a result of the altered pattern of price changes, the price *level*, the weighted average of all prices, will be lower. It is misleading, though, to associate the cost of price changes with a changing price level. Prices would have had to be changed in any event, although in a slightly different pattern.

Second, even if we allow ourselves to abstract from individual price changes and think in terms of price levels, an elastically supplied currency will not eliminate the need for costly price adjustments. Consider, for instance, a growing economy in which the real rate of interest is declining. Which price level should the monetary authority keep constant: the consumer price level, the factor price level, or the general price level (which includes prices of both consumer goods and factors of production)? If the consumer price level is kept constant, then factor prices will have to be continually adjusted upward as the rate of interest falls; if the factor price level is kept constant, then the prices of consumer goods will have to be continually adjusted downward; and if the general price level is kept constant, then the prices of both factors of production and consumer goods will have to be continually adjusted so as to reflect the declining interest rate. There is no price level whose constancy will eliminate the necessity for economy-wide adjustments in individual prices.

Third, the alleged price-adjustment costs of a gold standard are identified by comparing the gold standard as it actually operates with a paper standard as it ideally operates. Such comparisons never provide a sound basis for choosing between alternative institutional arrangements. The comparison assumes away all the relevant costs of a paper standard. If paper standards were administered by angelic monetary authorities whose sole objective was to minimize money-induced disequilibrium, the choice between a gold standard and a paper standard would be much less consequential than it actually is. But actual paper standards have price-adjustment costs too. And as history teaches, the magnitude and costliness of upward price adjustments under a paper standard dwarf the magnitude and costliness of downward price adjustments under a gold standard.[19]

The Unavoidable Resource Costs of Money

In the preceding section the contention was made that resource costs are doubly irrelevant to the issue of alternative monetary standards. Total costs, which are poorly proxied by resource costs, are the appropriate bases for comparison. This section establishes the double irrelevancy by showing that while resource costs are only a fraction of total costs, they constitute a part of total costs that the economy incurs whether on a gold standard or a paper standard. That is, the resource costs of gold constitute a part of the costs of both standards but all of the costs of neither standard. These costs, then, cannot be costs that influence the choice between the two monetary standards.

The effectiveness of the resource-cost argument against the gold standard rests on the popular perception that the activities of mining gold, refining it, casting it into bars or minting it into coins, storing it, and guarding it are collectively wasteful activities and the implicit assumption that if the gold standard were supplanted by a paper standard, these activities would cease. But making the implicit assumption explicit is enough to demonstrate its falsity. The imposition of a paper standard does not cause gold to lose its monetary value. To believe otherwise is to hold the naive view that the state can repeal the laws of economics. Gold continues to be mined, refined, cast or minted, stored, and guarded; the resource costs continue to be incurred. In fact, a paper standard administered by an irresponsible monetary authority may drive the monetary value of gold so high that more resource costs are incurred under the paper standard than would have been incurred under a gold standard. Market processes operating since antiquity have identified gold as the premier monetary commodity, and until the market's adoption of an alternative standard causes the value of gold to fall to a level that reflects only the nonmonetary uses of gold, these resource costs cannot be avoided.

There is a certain asymmetry in the cost comparison that turns the resource-cost argument against paper standards. When an irresponsible monetary authority begins to overissue paper money, market participants begin to hoard gold, which stimulates the gold-mining industry and drives up the resource costs. But when new discoveries of gold are made, market participants do not begin to hoard paper or to set up printing presses for the issue of unbacked currency. Gold is a good substitute for an officially instituted paper money, but paper is not a good substitute for an officially recognized metallic money. Because of this asymmetry, the resource costs incurred by the state in its efforts to impose a paper standard on the economy and manage the supply of paper money could be avoided if the state would simply recognize gold as money. These costs, then, can be counted against the paper standard.

As I suggested earlier, resource-cost comparisons that favor paper over gold are comparisons between real-world gold standards and fictitious paper standards.[20] Typically, the alternatives considered are strictly nonconformable: they consist of a market *process* that gives rise to the use of gold as the medium of exchange and an *outcome* that no known process can bring about. Wouldn't the world be a better place to live if there were no monetary value attached to gold (or to silver, copper, or ...) and if the monetary authority were constitutionally bound to increase the issue of paper money at a relatively slow, fixed, and fore-known rate? Wouldn't the world be an even better place to live if there were some other monetary commodity, a commodity which was relatively scarce, which could not be extracted by any known mining technique, but which was costlessly coughed up by nature at a slow and steady rate in locations that were experiencing economic growth? These worlds can be imagined to look just like the one that we actually live in—minus the resource costs of gold. Imagining such worlds may provide the basis for bad science fiction, but they are no basis at all for devising monetary theories or for choosing among alternative institutional arrangements.

A Constant Price Level versus Monetary Stability

The assumption of a constant price level has a history that is both long and wide. Over the years theorists representing diverse schools of thought have invoked this assumption in their effort to abstract from monetary influences on the course of economic activity, and they have adopted as a self-evident truth the notion that a constant price level is the hallmark of monetary stability. The significance of a constant price level for both theory and policy has been taken to be so obvious and self-evident that the literature is virtually devoid of attempts to defend these common practices. Yet a sampling of the many writers who do not question this assumption, and of the few who do, exposes the assumption as the Achilles' heel of the popular stance against the gold standard and of many other theoretical pronouncements and policy prescriptions.

Hayek noted in the early 1930s that an unaccountable preeminence of the constant price level characterized the writings of such monetary notables as Gustav Cassel and A.C. Pigou.[21] That a country should regulate its currency so as to achieve a constant price level appeared to Cassel as the "simplest assumption." If a country's currency were so regulated, money would exert no influence of its own, according to Pigou. The idea that an equality between economic growth and monetary growth is "natural" and that money whose growth rate satisfies this equality is "neutral" had become commonplace by the end of the twenties. The general acceptance of this idea eliminated the need for a theoretical justification.

The assumed relevance and desirability of a constant price level are incorporated in later decades in the writings of U.S. economists. In the early 1950s Clark Warburton included in his list of assumptions that underlie monetary theory the need for monetary growth to accommodate real economic growth. "[A]s a result of [population growth, technological developments, and increasing labor productivity] and of the stability of customs (such as the periodicity of income payments) which affect the rate of circulation of money, the economy needs for equilibrium a continuous increase in the quantity of money."[22] Following suit, Friedman assumed "for convenience" that a stable price level of final products is the objective of policy.[23] (It is both revealing and disquieting to note that Friedman's estimate of the resource costs of a gold standard discussed earlier in this chapter depends critically upon an assumption that was made for the sake of convenience.)

In the late 1960s Friedman reaffirmed that he "simply took it for granted, in line with a long tradition and near-consensus in the profession, that a stable level of prices of final products was a desirable objective."[24] The purpose of the article that contains this statement was to replace the assumed optimum of a constant price level with a theoretically derived optimum. After identifying costs and benefits of a changing price level, Friedman, following standard microeconomic procedures, set the marginal costs equal to the marginal benefits and solved for the optimal, or welfare-maximizing, rate of change in the price level. It turned out that with an assumed rate of economic growth of 3 or 4 percent a year, a decline in prices of 4 or 5 percent per year would maximize economic welfare.[25] At this rate of price deflation, the marginal gains associated with the deflation-induced increase in real cash holdings would just be offset by the nearly negligible marginal costs of increasing the supply of money. (These results apply to an economy using fiat currency. If gold were used instead, the marginal costs of extraction would cause the optimal rate of price deflation to be somewhat higher.)

From the outset Friedman failed fully to persuade even himself of the merits of his theoretically derived optimum. He ended the article with "A Final Schizophrenic Note" in which he teetered between endorsing a monetary rule that would optimize welfare as suggested by his theory and endorsing a monetary rule that would maintain a constant price level. In retrospect Friedman's calculations can be seen as a curious and contrived exercise in the application of marginalism. But today his arguments ring hollow. The unquestioned assumption of the desirability of a constant price level has regained its former status in discussions of monetary policy.

Economists of the Austrian school have always held the minority view that stable money and a constant price level are two different things.[26] At root their case is a very simple one. It requires only the most cursory consideration of what goes on behind the aggregates and the averages of the more orthodox monetary theory. It is true that productivity gains increase the level of output and thereby exert downward pressure on the level of prices. An offsetting increase in the total quantity of money can exert upward pressure and thereby preserve a constant price level. But productivity gains are themselves not neutral with respect to the composition of output. Economic growth does not consist of an across-the-board increase in the quantity of goods produced. It consists instead of increases in the quantities of some goods and decreases in the quantities of other goods, improvements in the quality of some goods, and the introduction of new goods. Growth-induced changes in the pattern of output are accompanied by corresponding changes in the pattern of prices. The fact that the price level calculated on the basis of the new pattern is lower than the price level calculated on the basis of the old pattern is strictly incidental. To the extent that each individual change in the pattern of prices can be attributed to nonmonetary factors, the issue of monetary nonneutrality does not arise despite the fall in the price level.[27]

The Austrians go on to point out that if an increase in the supply of money is brought about so that economic growth can be "accommodated," the effects of the monetary injection on prices will be compounding rather than counteracting. Economic growth coupled with monetary growth may allow for a constant price level, but the pattern of prices will be affected in one way by the economic growth and in some other way by the monetary growth. Although it can be imagined that the increase in the supply of money affects only the price level, this lone effect cannot, because of the very nature of money, be actualized. Actual monetary injections, whether in the presence or the absence of economic growth, are always nonneutral.[28] They always have their own relative-price effects which, in turn, have effects on the pattern of output. A constant price level, then, is neither an appropriate assumption for devising monetary theories nor the most appropriate goal of monetary policies.

In current debate the goal of a constant price level enjoys a certain popularity for two reasons. Both have at least some merit, but neither constitutes a telling case against the gold standard. The first reason has to do with political feasibility. Some may argue that the prospects of persuading the central bank to adopt a constant price level as its goal are better than the prospects of persuading it to surrender totally to the dictates of a commodity money. The adoption of such a goal would at least be a step in the right direction, and it would not preclude a further step to a commodity standard if such a step were to prove desirable and feasible. But those who now favor the gold standard do not expect that the central bank will adopt a goal of a constant price level. In fact, they believe that the central bank's unwillingness to do so—or otherwise to behave responsibly—goes a long way toward proving the desirability of a commodity standard. And they believe that the question of which sort of monetary institution is the most desirable should be kept separate from the question of the political feasibility of bringing about the needed institutional change.[29]

The second reason for the popularity of this goal derives from money's role as a unit of value and its relationship in this regard to other units such as units of length and units of weight.[30] The analogy between the need for invariant units of length and weight and the need for an invariant unit of value is appealing. Carpenters would not fare well in their trade if they had to use measuring devices that expand and shrink on their own; truck drivers would experience an increased dread of weigh stations if they had to wonder how heavy a pound is today. The images conjured up by examples of this sort drive the point home. To be serviceable, units of length, weight, and value must be invariant over time. The analogy is persuasive and may be just the right medicine for those who advocate inflation or who advocate artificially cheap credit even if the ultimate result is inflation.

But for the advocates of sound money, there is more to be learned from the sense in which the analogy does not hold than the sense in which it does. Invariance can be achieved for units of length and weight but not for units of value. Modern attempts to discover or create an invariant unit of value (in the form of multiple-commodity standards, indexation schemes, and the like) represent a throwback to the old pre-marginalist, presubjectivist classical economics. They require that we unlearn the lessons implicit in Ricardo's fruitless search.[31]

This point can be driven home with an analogy of a different sort. (It takes an analogy to beat an analogy.) A monetary commodity is more like a reference commodity, a base point, or benchmark, than like a measuring unit. An immutable reference *value* for gauging all other values has as its physical analog an immutable reference *point* in the cosmos. Some might argue that the earth cannot serve as such a reference point, because the earth is revolving around the sun, which is revolving around the center of the Milky Way galaxy, which is moving through the universe. An immutable reference point has to be independent of all these movements. Different schemes for locating such a point, which take into account all the relative locations of all the heavenly bodies, might be proposed. But reflection will reveal that the immutable reference point is as useless as it is illusive. The most relevant reference point is the point where cosmic developments have put us. And so it is with the reference value. The most relevant reference commodity is the monetary commodity that market processes have given us. Once gold emerged as the world's monetary commodity, it became irrelevant that certain prices or prices in general may be "unstable" with respect to some other reference value or some index of values. If undisturbed by political schemes, gold should be regarded as a stable money until the market process itself, for whatever reasons, begins to favor some other commodity as a value reference.[32]

The different opponents of the gold standard have radically different reasons for wanting to reject gold as money. Some want to harness the monetary forces and put the reins in the hands of government; others want to nullify the monetary forces that are inherent in any commodity standard. The former like to think of monetary stability as those monetary arrangements that result in full employment; the latter like to think of monetary stability as those monetary arrangements that result in a constant price level. Proponents of the gold standard hold that neither full employment nor a constant price level is an appropriate goal of government policy. Nor is either of these goals consistent with monetary stability. And achieving the goal of stable money, which may well result in both fuller employment and a more nearly constant price level than would otherwise be possible, requires only that the government refrain from interfering with the commodity money chosen by the market.

Concluding Remarks

Opponents of the gold standard calculate the costs of gold in dollars and cents and report their calculations as a percentage of the economy's output. The intended interpretation is clear: but for the costs of gold, the economy would have had an output that much greater. Proponents of the gold standard would be ill-advised to respond with a cost figure of their own. If the true costs of a gold standard could be calculated at all, it would have to take into account the monetary instability associated with alternative standards and the consequent loss of output. But incorporating these considerations would undoubtedly cause the cost figures to turn negative. The gold standard has net benefits, not net costs. An appreciation of these benefits, but not a precise quantitative estimate, can best be gained by comparisons of historical episodes which are illustrative of economic performance under a gold standard and economic performance under a paper standard. The superiority of the former in comparison to the latter constitutes the net benefits of the gold standard.[33]

Ultimately, the cost of any action, commodity, or institution is the alternative action, commodity, or institution forgone. The opportunity cost is the only cost that counts. The cost of one institution is forgoing some other institution; the cost of the gold standard is forgoing a paper standard; the cost of sound money is forgoing unsound money.

Notes

1. Carl Menger, "On the Origin of Money," *Economic Journal* 2 (June 1892):239–55. Also see Menger, *Principles of Economics*, translated and edited by James Dingwall and Bert F. Hoselitz (Glencoe, Ill.: Free Press, 1950), pp. 257–62.

2. One early list of such characteristics includes (1) utility and value, (2) portability, (3) indestructability, (4) homogeneity, (5) divisibility, (6) stability of value, and (7) cognizability. William Stanley Jevons, *Money and the Mechanism of Exchange* (New York: D. Appleton, 1882), p. 31. It might be noted that characteristics 1 and 6 of Jevons's list are strongly reinforced as the particular commodity so characterized emerges as the medium of exchange.

3. Ibid., p. 41. Jevons lists in order: gold, silver, copper, tin, lead, and iron. Also see Ludwig von Mises, *The Theory of Money and Credit*, translated by H.E. Batson (New Haven: Yale University Press, 1953), pp. 30–34.

4. Milton Friedman, "Should There Be an Independent Monetary Authority?," in Leland B. Yeager, ed., *In Search of a Monetary Constitution* (Cambridge: Harvard University Press, 1962), p. 228.

5. F.A. Hayek, "The Results of Human Action but not of Human Design," in Hayek, *Studies in Philosophy, Politics and Economics* (New York: Simon and Schuster, 1969), p. 104.

6. Ibid. Language and money are probably the two most striking examples of social phenomena that have "arisen from man's actions without his design."

7. Ludwig von Mises, *On the Manipulation of Money and Credit*, translated by Bettina Bien Graves and edited by Percy L. Graves, Jr. (Dobbs Ferry, N.Y.: Free Market Books, 1978), p. 80. Also see Mises, *Human Action*, 3rd rev. ed. (Chicago: Henry Regnery, 1966), pp. 471–76.

8. John Maynard Keynes, *The General Theory of Employment, Interest, and Money* (New York: Harcourt, Brace and World, 1964), pp. 229–36. Keynes is very clear on this point: "It is interesting to notice that the characteristic which has been traditionally supposed to render gold especially suitable for use as a standard of value, namely, its inelasticity of supply, turns out to be precisely the characteristic which is at the bottom of the trouble." This statement follows the more fanciful account of the trouble with gold: "Unemployment develops, that is to say, because people want the moon;—men cannot be employed when the object of their desire (i.e. money) is something which cannot be produced and the demand for which cannot be readily choked off. There is no remedy but to

persuade the public that green cheese is practically the same thing and to have a green cheese factory (i.e. a central bank) under public control." Ibid., pp. 235–36.

9. For an account of the clay-brick standard first proposed by C.O. Hardy, see James M. Buchanan, "Predictability: the Criterion of Monetary Constitutions," in Yeager, *In Search of a Monetary Constitution,* pp. 155–83.

10. Milton Friedman, "Commodity-Reserve Currency," in *Essays in Positive Economics* (Chicago: University of Chicago Press, 1953), pp. 204–50. In his discussion of the supply elasticities of alternative monetary commodities, Friedman points out the disadvantages of an elasticity greater than zero (pp. 209–10) as well as the disadvantages of an elasticity less than infinity (pp. 210–14). The idea that the use of a monetary commodity whose supply elasticity is greater than zero involves "waste" has a long history and was endorsed by the classical economists, including Smith and Ricardo.

11. Ibid., p. 210. Also, see Milton Friedman, *A Program for Monetary Stability* (New York: Fordham University Press, 1959), p. 5.

12. These estimates are from Friedman's "Commodity-Reserve Currency," which was originally published in 1951. The high resource costs were to become even higher by the end of the decade when Friedman offered a new estimate in his *Program for Monetary Stability.* On the basis of a slightly higher rate of economic growth, he estimated that about 2.5 percent of the economy's output, or $8 billion per year, would have to be devoted to the procurement of additional quantities of the monetary commodity.

13. Allan H. Meltzer, "Monetary Reform in an Uncertain Environment," *The Cato Journal* 3, no. 1 (Spring 1983):93–112. Meltzer's updated estimate is found on p. 105. This particular estimating procedure, in which the estimate of the resource costs of gold is always some multiple of the economy's growth rate, gives rise to an interesting paradox. If mismanaged paper money causes so much economic discoordination that the growth rate drops to zero, the estimated resource costs of maintaining a gold standard would also drop to zero; but if the adoption of the now-inexpensive gold standard creates economic stability and fosters new growth, maintaining the gold standard would once again become too costly.

14. Friedman, "Commodity-Reserve Currency," p. 210; *A Program for Monetary Stability,* p. 5.

15. This point has been emphasized by Ronald Coase: "It would seem desirable to use [an opportunity-cost] approach when dealing with questions of economic policy and to compare the total product yielded by alternative social arrangements." Coase, "The Problem of Social Cost," *Journal of Law and Economics* 3 (October 1960):43.

16. It would be a gross misrepresentation, of course, to add the costs that are incurred as a result of an assumed inelasticity of the supply of gold to the resource costs that are based on an assumed perfect elasticity.

17. Arguments of this sort have their roots in the writings of Clark Warburton. See Warburton, "The Monetary Disequilibrium Hypothesis," in Warburton, *Depression, Inflation, and Monetary Policy, Selected Papers, 1945-1953,* (Baltimore: The Johns Hopkins Press, 1966), pp. 25–35. Also, see Leland B. Yeager, "Stable Money and Free-Market Currencies," *Cato Journal* 3, no. 1 (Spring 1983):305–26.

18. A more thorough discussion of the relevance of a constant price level is offered later in chapter 4.

19. For historical perspectives on gold and paper, see Murray N. Rothbard, *What has Government Done to Our Money?* (A Pine Tree Publication, 1963), pp. 27–49; Ron Paul and Lewis Lehrman, *The Case for Gold: A Minority Report of the U.S. Gold Commission* (Washington, D.C.: Cato Institute, 1982), pp. 17–142; and Alan Reynolds, "Why Gold?," *The Cato Journal 3*, no. 1 (Spring 1983):211–32.

20. Again, it was Ronald Coase who sensitized the profession to "the usual treatment of [problems of social cost in which] the analysis proceeds in terms of a comparison between a state of laissez faire and some kind of ideal world." He went on to point out that "very little analysis is required to show that an ideal world is better than a state of laissez faire unless the definitions of a state of laissez faire and an ideal world happen to be the same." Coase, "The Problem of Social Cost," p. 43. Harold Demsetz has elaborated on the differences between the "nirvana approach" (which is implicitly adopted by many critics of the gold standard) and the "comparative-institutions approach" (which is adopted in the present paper). Demsetz, "Information and Efficiency: Another Viewpoint," *Journal of Law and Economics 12* (April 1969):1–22.

21. F.A. Hayek, *Prices and Production*, 2nd ed. (New York: Augustus M. Kelley, 1967), p. 107.

22. Warburton, "The Monetary Disequilibrium Hypothesis," p. 28. Warburton notes that this assumption "pervaded so much economic literature of the nineteenth century and early part of the twentieth that supporting documentary references seem superfluous." Ibid., p. 29.

23. Friedman, "Commodity-Reserve Currency," p. 210.

24. Milton Friedman, "The Optimum Quantity of Money," in *The Optimum Quantity of Money and Other Essays* (Chicago: Aldine, 1969), p. 48.

25. Ibid., p. 46.

26. Hayek, *Prices and Production*, pp. 105–31; Mises, *Human Action*, pp. 219–28 and *passim*; Mises, *On the Manipulation of Money and Credit*, pp. 1–49; and Mises, *Theory of Money and Credit*, pp. 108–69.

27. Mises, *Theory of Money and Credit*, p. 123. Mises maintains a first-order distinction between "two sorts of determinants of the exchange-value that connects money and other economic goods; those that exercise their effect on the money side of the ratio and those that exercise their effect on the commodity side." Only the effects of the first-mentioned sort are relevant to the issue of monetary neutrality.

28. Mises, *Human Action*, p. 418. "The notion of a neutral money is no less contradictory than that of a money of stable purchasing power. Money without a driving force of its own would not, as people assume, be a perfect money; it would not be money at all." The fact that money is not neutral is the common denominator of the monetary theories of Mises, Hayek, and others who have written in the Austrian tradition.

29. Friedman has enunciated this maxim but has not always abided by it. "The role of the economist in discussions of public policy seems to me to be to prescribe what should be done in the light of what can be done, politics aside, and not to predict what is 'politically feasible' and then to recommend it." Milton

Friedman, "Comments on Monetary Policy," in *Essays in Positive Economics* (Chicago: University of Chicago Press, 1953), p. 264. William Hutt, who is critical of the Friedman maxim, recommends that the economist take political considerations into account, but only if such considerations are made explicit. This, he argues, is the business of old-style "political economy." William H. Hutt, *Politically Impossible* ... ? (London: Institute of Economic Affairs, 1971), pp. 22–27.

30. Yeager, "Stable Money and Free-Market Currencies," pp. 305–308.

31. "The search for a stable unit of account is ultimately the search for an invariant standard of value, the quixotic goal of classical political economy." Gerald P. O'Driscoll, Jr., "A Free-Market Money: Comment on Yeager," *The Cato Journal* 3, no. 1 (Spring 1983):328.

32. "Economic calculation does not require monetary stability in the sense in which this term is used by the champions of the stabilization movement. The fact that rigidity in the monetary unit's purchasing power is unthinkable and unrealizable does not impair the methods of economic calculation. What economic calculation requires is a monetary system whose functioning is not sabotaged by government interference." Mises, *Human Action*, p. 223. It should be noted that the dramatic fluctuations in the value of gold in recent years do not imply that gold is no longer a viable monetary commodity. Quite the contrary, volatile shifts in the demand for hard money are a reflection of the instability of our present monetary institution. The paper money is losing *its* viability. See Mises, *On the Manipulation of Money and Credit*, pp. 76–77.

33. Historical studies are cited in note 19, above.

5

Gold and the International Monetary System: The Contribution of Michael A. Heilperin

Joseph T. Salerno

In considering some of the important issues raised by an international monetary system based on gold, I have chosen to focus on the works of an undeservedly obscure economist, Michael A. Heilperin.[1] There are, I believe, a number of compelling reasons for proceeding in this manner.

First and foremost, in his long, prolific, and distinguished career spanning almost four decades (1931–1968), Heilperin was an outspoken critic of fiat money inflation and an uncompromising defender of the gold standard. Practically alone among professional economists after World War II, he advocated a return to the relatively hard money, pre-1914, or "classical" gold standard and, because of the influential positions he held, was able to gain a hearing for his views among the leading monetary policymakers of the Western world.[2] Nevertheless, his writings have been altogether neglected, not only by mainstream economists but also by the growing number of contemporary proponents of a gold-based international monetary system. This is particularly unfortunate since Heilperin was especially inclined to formulate his progold arguments and proposals in the light of modern policy considerations. It is therefore with a view to valuable instruction as well as to redressing a glaring doctrinal oversight that I draw attention to Heilperin's contributions.

A second important consideration is that Heilperin kept sound classical balance-of-payments and exchange rate analysis alive during an era that had forsaken monetary explanations of deficits and depreciating exchange rates in favor of Keynesian explanations that emphasized "real" causes of balance-of-payments and exchange rate phenomena such as

I wish to acknowledge Dr. Murray N. Rothbard, New York Polytechnic Institute, for first drawing my attention to Heilperin's works and Dr. Lawrence H. White, New York University, for his comments on a draft of this chapter.

"technology gaps," "perverse foreign exchange market elasticities," "over-absorption of national income," and "foreign trade multipliers." In this respect, Heilperin stands as an important though heretofore unacknowledged forerunner of the modern monetary approach to the balance of payments.

A careful study of Heilperin's writings is instructive on a third account. Like the more famous advocate of the gold standard, Jacques Rueff,[3] Heilperin was long an opponent of the gold exchange standard and presented insightful and prophetic critiques of the system, especially as it operated during the Bretton Woods era (1946–1971). His prophecies of its eventual and inevitable collapse, though derided when they were initially advanced, were right on the money in light of later developments. This serves as an invaluable illustration of the usefulness of sound deductive economic theory in the forecasting of the evolution and devolution of broad patterns of economic activities. Moreover, Heilperin's objections to the gold exchange standard have contemporary relevance in view of the support for a return to a system of the Bretton Woods type that has been voiced by a number of prominent supply siders and other advocates of a monetary "price rule."[4]

Lastly, contemporary proponents of a genuine gold standard can hopefully learn from the damaging mistakes committed by Heilperin in his characterization and defense of the international gold standard. His errors in this respect stem from a fundamental misconception, shared with most modern economic theorists and policymakers, of the nature and evolution of money and monetary institutions. It was this underlying "constructivist" approach to money that led Heilperin to propose a "semiautomatic" or "managed" gold bullion standard in which the government is accorded the role of money manager. The unfortunate fact is that proposals like Heilperin's have lent credibility to the distorted portrayal of the gold standard as nothing more than a government price-fixing scheme carried out on a grand scale.

The Gold Standard and the "Mechanism of Reequilibrium"

By the advent of the Bretton Woods era, most economists had come to reject the Humean, classical view that there exists a market mechanism that operates automatically to preserve and restore equilibrium in a nation's balance of payments. In the then prevailing post-Keynesian balance-of-payments theories, money was assigned a passive role as an item that served to balance the inevitable mismatchings between debit and credit items in a nation's foreign trade and capital accounts.

The Keynesians believed that the direction and magnitude of international money flows are wholly and completely determined by the decisions made in the "real" sector of the economy—that is, in the goods and capital markets.[5] Since these decisions, regarding where and how much to buy, sell, and invest, are those of countless households and businesses operating independently of one another, there is no reason to expect that, in the case of a given nation, an equilibrium would ever tend to be spontaneously struck between the aggregate foreign payments and receipts of the nation's residents. There are two important implications of the Keynesian perspective on the balance of payments: first, that government policies of one sort or another are necessary to prevent the development of chronic disequilibria in a nation's external payments position; and, second, that therefore the relatively unregulated classical gold standard is an unstable and unsustainable international monetary regime.

It was in this intellectual atmosphere that Heilperin forcefully and cogently reaffirmed the doctrine of David Hume and the classical economists that, under an international gold standard, there exist potent market forces which operate spontaneously to effect a speedy and precise adjustment of balance-of-payments disequilibria. Implicit in the classical doctrine is the recognition that money does indeed play an active and essential part in the balance of payments and, in particular, that people make their sale, purchase, and investment decisions with an eye to acquiring or maintaining a desired level of money balances. A most important implication of this view is that inflationary monetary policy gums up and eventually destroys the workings of the automatic balance-of-payments adjustment mechanism. Let us take a closer look at the balance-of-payments adjustment process as it was understood by Heilperin to operate under the international gold standard.

What Heilperin terms the "mechanism of reequilibrium" is activated whenever a discrepancy begins to develop between the payments and the receipts that result from a nation's foreign transactions, both commercial and financial. Heilperin analyzes this mechanism in the simplest case of an international gold currency in which "gold is the only money in circulation in the various countries."[6] Such an "all-gold currency" or "simple specie currency" is characterized as one "where no national monetary policy exists at all."[7]

To illustrate the operation of the equilibration mechanism under this monetary regime, let us suppose that a deficit develops in a nation's overall balance of payments. The immediate consequence of this development is an outflow of gold abroad. As Heilperin notes, "this amounts to a contraction of the circulating medium in the country losing gold and to an expansion in the other country (or countries). In consequence, prices tend to fall in the former and rise in the latter country, which discourages the former country's imports and encourages her exports, while the reverse happens in the latter country."[8] These relative price movements tend automatically to restore equilibrium in the deficit nation's balance of payments.

Now this is an outline of the familiar price-specie-flow mechanism associated with the names of Hume and Ricardo. There is another factor, however, besides the alterations of relative prices, that facilitates the automatic equilibration of the balance of payments. This is quite simply the direct effect on spending, on both domestic and foreign goods and services, which is caused by a flow of money from one nation to another. For example, the reduction in the money supply in the deficit nation would, ceteris paribus, cause a contraction in the money incomes of its residents, and this would directly induce a decline in their demands for both domestic and foreign products. The same sequence of events would occur, except in the opposite direction, in the surplus nation, where the money stock and hence money incomes are expanding. "Thus the country whose balance of payments shows a deficit would buy less goods of the other country (assuming two countries in presence) while the latter country would increase her importations from the former." In short, "changes in demand schedules, brought about by payments from country to country, affect trade between these countries in a way which tends to re-establish equilibrium of international payments...."[9]

The latter effect is known today as the "real balance" effect and is especially, if not exclusively, emphasized in the modern monetary approach to the balance of payments. Heilperin's discussion of this effect is not completely satisfactory, however, because it does not take explicit account of individuals' desired holdings of cash balances.[10] Nevertheless, Heilperin's overall analysis of the adjustment mechanism does partake of the spirit of the monetary approach in its illumination of the automatic character of the interrelations subsisting among the balance of payments, the supply of money, and aggregate money income and expenditure. For example, Heilperin speaks of the "changes which disequilibrium in international payments brings forth in the various national money markets. These changes must, even in the absence of any special policy, alter the structure of international trade and of internal demand."[11]

In summary: "Under a system of simple specie currency, the deficit of the balance of payments causes a change in the supply of money in the countries concerned, and thus affects trade (a) directly via shifts in demand schedules brought about by changes in the supply of money [the direct-spending or real-balance effect]; and (b) indirectly through price changes resulting from movements of specie from country to country [the relative-price effect]."[12] The equilibrating effect of the deficit upon the supply of money persists until the deficit itself is completely eradicated and balance-of-payments equilibrium restored.

While disequilibria in the balance of payments are thus automatically adjusted in the textbook abstraction of the 100 percent gold standard, the classical gold standard requires that the automatic adjustment mechanism be supplemented by government monetary policy designed to induce reequilibrium. The implementation of such policy is necessitated by certain institutional features of the classical gold standard. Most significantly, under this monetary system, the nation's stock of monetary gold tends to be centralized in the hands of its central bank, which employs the gold as reserves for its own note and deposit liabilities.

The central bank's notes and deposit balances are held by the public, including private banks, and are legally convertible into gold upon demand. Since a deficit balance of payments must be financed by gold shipments to foreigners by members of the public, deficits have a direct impact on the stock of gold reserves of the central bank. To arrest the deficit, the central bank is constrained to raise its discount rate, thereby constricting its loans to private banks. As Heilperin notes, the policy of raising the discount or "bank" rate has a "twofold effect upon the monetary situation: (1) the increase of the bank rate tends to reduce the portion of monetary circulation which is backed not by gold but by commercial paper, and thus tends to restore the percentage of gold cover of the total amount of central bank money; (2) that same increase of the rate of interest tends to attract short-term funds from abroad."[13]

The alteration in the national money stock effected by the contractionary discount-rate policy therefore serves to reinforce the relative-price and direct-spending (or demand-shift) effects of the automatic mechanism and thus to hasten the adjustment of the balance of payments. Furthermore, the influx of short-term funds from abroad in response to higher domestic interest rates directly reduces the magnitude of the deficit.

Heilperin concludes that, under the classical gold standard, balance-of-payments adjustment depends crucially upon the monetary authorities adopting the appropriate policies:

> It is clear that, in order to obtain a new equilibrium in international payments, policies must be adopted which will in effect stimulate exports and discourage imports of the country (or countries) in deficit, while the opposite effects must be obtained in the country (or countries) experiencing a surplus. The appropriate policy is one of credit restrictions in the country in deficit and of credit expansion in the country having a surplus. This may be obtained by modifying appropriately the bank rate or by applying open-market policies aiming at the same results.[14]

Mindful of the consistently perverse and inflationary application of open-market operations by the British and U.S. central banks in the

1920s, Heilperin is quick to warn against the great potential for the abuse and destruction of the gold standard that characterizes such a potent tool of government monetary manipulation: "Of course when resorting to open-market operations one must apply them in a proper way; that is in order to restrict the monetary circulation in the country in deficit and to expand it in the other one. In actual practice this method has been all too frequently used to hamper rather than to help the mechanism of adjustment in its action; the typical example is that of central banks *buying* securities when gold is flowing out of the country, thus counteracting the necessary restriction of circulating medium."[15]

In fact it was this perverse application of open market operations, in the service of the Fisherian-monetarist desideratum of price level stability, that brought down the attenuated gold exchange standard of the 1920s:

> The idea of stabilizing the "price level" led to the adoption of open-market operations of a type exactly opposed to those which would have been required for the maintenance of a long-run equilibrium in international payments. As a result of the policies adopted the monetary circulation was prevented from falling and the bank rate from rising in the countries losing gold, while the monetary circulation was kept up and the bank rate down in countries receiving an inflow of the metal. Under these conditions mechanisms of adjustment of balances of payments could not, of course, work properly, and deep-rooted maladjustments inevitably developed.
>
> The doom of the "new gold standard" was brought about by the obsession of an impending "scarcity" of gold and by the attempt to achieve price stability *against* the "rules of the game."[16]

In repeatedly emphasizing the proposition that "most balance-of-payments difficulties are due to national inflations,"[17] Heilperin anticipates another important insight of the modern monetary approach. This is that a chronic deficit in a nation's external payments account can only arise when there is a continuous re-creation of excess cash balances in the domestic money market via monetary inflation. In this situation, the persistent efforts of the public to rid themselves of excess balances results in a net import of goods and securities from abroad and a net efflux of gold reserves. Balance-of-payments equilibrium will be restored only when money creation ceases and domestic money balances attain desired levels.

Because he conceived monetary factors to play a basic role in determining the balance of payments, it is no surprise that Heilperin was one of the few economists to dissent from the prevailing view that the dollar shortage experienced by Europe after World War II was due to certain structural or real factors that would persist indefinitely. These included the technological backwardness of Europe relative to the United States, the wartime destruction of Europe's export markets and industries, the great "need" for imports to sustain Europe's reconstruction of its basic industries and infrastructure, and other explanations.

One of the many economists to present the structuralist interpretation of European deficits was the leading American Keynesian of the day, Alvin Hansen. According to Hansen:

> The fundamental problem of dollar scarcity remains more or less an inscrutable enigma.... It is partly a matter of technology—the immense superiority of American mass-production techniques in a wide range of products eagerly sought for in the modern world, including automobiles, electrical appliances, machinery, etc. It is in some measure related to the high American tariff. It is partly due to the strong preference...of the mass of American consumers for American-made products, continually reinforced by advertising campaigns. Domestic goods produced under the conditions of monopolistic competition or oligopoly are not likely to be supplanted in volume by the inroads of foreign competition. It is partly a matter of wrong valuation of many foreign currencies. And finally, it cannot be denied that the trade policies of many nations contribute to the imbalance.[18]

To Heilperin, on the other hand, the scarcity of dollars was due almost solely to continuing domestic inflations in the European nations in conjunction with pegged exchange rates that overvalued the depreciated European currencies relative to the dollar: "There can be no doubt that inflationary policies, combined with the pegging of exchange rates at artificial levels, have been responsible for a large part of the payment difficulties of the post-war years."[19]

In 1949 Heilperin argued that import restrictions and exchange controls would never succeed in remedying the unbalanced payments situation between the United States and Europe and that the only true remedy was for the European countries to return to a hard-money regime: "I am not at all sure that it is sound to discuss the problem of European reconstruction solely in terms of availability of so-called 'hard currencies,' that is to say principally of the dollar. Unless the European currencies are also made 'hard' through arresting inflations and restoring convertibility, the dollar shortage will, I am sure, never end."[20]

Heilperin's bold forecast was borne out when, in 1958, the governments of Western Europe abandoned most of their draconian restrictions on international trade and investment, brought their inflations to a halt, and reestablished unrestricted convertibility between their currencies and the dollar at realistic exchange rates. Almost immediately, the seemingly intractable dollar shortage melted away. In fact, a "dollar glut" shortly emerged that ultimately caused the demise of the Bretton Woods system.

This brings us to the second instance in which Heilperin used sound economic analysis as the basis for an accurate forecast of the effects of politicoeconomic institutions on the broad pattern of economic incentives and activities. In this case he argued that the gold exchange standard, which reemerged after the Second World War under the auspices of the Bretton Woods agreement, was an unstable international monetary system that would inevitably generate worldwide inflation and chronic balance-of-payments disequilibria.

The gold exchange standard was first adopted in the 1920s as a means of averting an impending world "gold scarcity," which was widely anticipated to result when the depreciated currencies of Europe were "stabilized" once again on a gold convertible basis. Since these currencies had been greatly inflated during World War I, the obvious and realistic solution was to admit openly the fact of past inflation and return to the gold standard at legally devalued parities—that is, at a higher "price" of gold in terms of the national currency. Unfortunately, it was decided at the Genoa Conference of 1922 to institute convertibility at the prewar parities but for most nations to hold gold convertible "key currencies" as monetary reserves in order to economize on gold. Great Britain and the United States were to remain on the gold standard proper, and the pound and dollar were to be employed as the key currencies. From 1925 to 1928 the gold exchange standard was established in country after country.[21]

Heilperin was one of the first to identify the inherently inflationary nature of this scheme. In 1939 he wrote that this arrangement entails "inflationary tendencies of a world-wide character."[22]

This follows from the fact that,

> If monetary reserves of certain countries are held in the form of ordinary balances with commercial banks of the gold-standard countries, a double expansion can take place on the basis of existing stocks of monetary gold: In the gold-standard country there exists the usual "inverted pyramid of credit": gold, bank notes, demand deposits ("bank money"); now a part of the top stratum of that pyramid can become the basic stratum of another such pyramid in a country on the gold exchange standard. Every short-term credit made by a gold-standard country to one on the gold exchange standard may thus become the basis of credit expansion in the latter *without* causing the least credit contraction in the former![23]

Heilperin concluded that the intended economization of gold

> can only occur if the gold exchange standard is made an instrument of inflation.... All goes very well as long as the effects of inflation do not

make themselves felt and as long as countries on the gold exchange standard do not avail themselves of the right to convert their foreign balances into gold. But since both these things are sooner or later likely to happen, the economy in the use of gold is associated with an increased instability of the monetary system.[24]

The gold exchange standard was thus "an adulterated verson of the gold standard," "a machine for perpetual inflation."[25] It was the employment of this machine to achieve the chimeric goal of price level stability that caused the inflationary boom of the 1920s and the subsequent Great Depression.[26] And it was "wrong economic diagnosis, compounded by bad semantics" that resulted in the blame for the depression and world monetary breakdown of the 1930s being laid at the doorstep of the classical gold standard. In fact, the gold exchange standard had "weakened the signalling system and the whole delicate mechanism that had brought equilibrium under the gold standard."[27]

After World War II Heilperin was one of the first economists, along with Rueff, to recognize that the gold exchange standard, with all its potential for monetary instability, had quietly reemerged under cover of the Bretton Woods system. In 1961 he sounded the alarm and predicted that the world monetary system was on the verge of imminent collapse:

> International monetary organization built in part on gold and in part on gold-convertible currencies—the Gold Exchange Standard—has proven highly dangerous in the interwar years and has slipped back into existence since the end of World War II. It promotes inflation in its optimistic or expanding phase, and deflation (even collapse) in its pessimistic or contracting phase. It tends to encourage balance-of-payments deficits— and to make them chronic—in countries whose currency is used as reserve currency abroad (because these countries do not pay off their deficits, which would result in the adoption of policy correctives, but merely build up a gold-convertible foreign indebtedness). The longer the expanding phase of the Gold Exchange Standard lasts, the greater foreign demand liabilities of the key-currency countries become, and the greater the risk of an international confidence crisis, of demands for massive gold payments, and of an eventual international monetary breakdown.
>
> If key-currency countries follow policies aimed at balanced external accounts, the supply of their currencies for reserve purposes diminishes. In fact, any gold exchange standard must come to an end quietly, through sound policies of key-currency countries, or chaotically, through a crisis of confidence in the key currencies and large demands for gold repayments.[28]

Despite the numerous political expedients implemented to avert it, the end for the Bretton Woods system came chaotically, as it went through a slow motion crash beginning in 1960 when the free market gold price temporarily broke above the official price and finally ending in 1971 when President Nixon officially "closed the gold window."[29]

It is instructive to note that Heilperin's verbal logical analysis of the mechanics and incentive structure of the gold exchange standard enabled him to make an accurate qualitative forecast or "pattern prediction"[30] regarding the type of economic phenomena that would evolve under this institution, namely inflation and perennial balance-of-payments disequilibria generated by the monetary policies of the key-currency country. In sharp contrast, the great majority of "empirical" mainstream economists during the 1960s steadfastly denied the inevitability or even the possibility of the collapse of such a hallowed and trusted institution as the Bretton Woods system.

The International Gold Standard and Domestic Economic Stability

As early as 1923 John Maynard Keynes declared that the choice of an international monetary regime involved an unpleasant dilemma. Keynes argued, "If...the external price-level lies outside our control, we must submit either to our own internal price-level or to our exchange being pulled about by external influences. If the external price-level is instable, we cannot keep both our own price-level, and our exchanges stable. And we are compelled to choose."[31]

In effect Keynes was contending that the operation of the mechanism by which international balances of payments are equilibrated under the gold standard regularly and necessarily subjects a nation to bouts of inflation or deflation. This characterization of the gold standard appeared to be confirmed by events when, in 1925, Britain reestablished convertibility of the pound and promptly experienced deflationary pressure on its economy. That Britain was able to offset such pressure by an "autonomous" monetary policy of reflation only after it abandoned the gold standard in 1931 served as further evidence of the veracity of Keynes's argument.

For Heilperin, however, the belief that the normal operation of the gold standard is inconsistent with domestic price stability is based on a number of serious errors of economic analysis and historical interpretation.

Thus, Heilperin considers the dilemma "more apparent than real," because "[i]t has its source in a rather oversimplified theory of the functioning of the gold standard."[32]

One of the most important aspects of this oversimplification involves the use of the concept of a national price level when discussing the functioning of the adjustment mechanism. As Heilperin points out, such "statistical constructions" seem

> to provide a comfortable way out of the perplexing multiplicity and heterogeneity presented by the economic world and the processes that are taking place therein....But the multiplicity does exist and by ignoring it one falls into erroneous or meaningless statements about the world and about economic processes. Averages more often conceal reality than reveal it and have to be used cautiously, even in homogeneous collections; but they are simply without meaning in collections that are not homogeneous. There is no such thing in the real economic world as the "general price level"; but what exists are prices, and it is the movements of prices and the changes in the structure of money values (including prices, incomes, debts) that are of real interest and of intense importance for the understanding of economic phenomena.[33]

Thus, by conducting analysis in terms of national price levels, one is naturally led to conclude that what is required, as in the case of a deficit, is a general "deflation" of the nation's price level. But this hides the fact that what is really needed to restore balance-of-payments equilibrium in a deficit situation is a decline of some particular prices, which hardly qualifies as a deflation in the usual sense of the term. It thus becomes evident that "[p]rice movements which enter into a process of adjustment of international payments are not likely to be of an amplitude which would seriously disturb economic activity and amount to a deflation (or inflation)."[34]

More important, it is highly inappropriate to use the terms "inflation" or "deflation" in describing the adjustment process under an international gold standard unless one is prepared to use the same terminology to explain the effects of any interlocal transfer of money. On this point Heilperin approvingly refers to the pathbreaking analysis of Friedrich A. Hayek.[35] According to Heilperin, the key to Hayek's analysis is the insight that the adjustment of balance-of-payments disturbances occurs via sequential processes of changes in individual prices, incomes, and expenditures, which operate without respect to imaginary national borders. The magnitude and even the direction of the change of a particular good's price does not depend, therefore, upon the nation in which the good is offered for sale. As Hayek explains:

> The important point in all this is that what incomes and what prices will have to be altered in consequence of the initial change will depend on whether and to what extent the value of a particular factor or service, directly or indirectly, depends on the particular change in demand which has occurred, and not whether it is inside or outside the same

"currency area." We can see this more clearly if we picture the series of successive changes of money incomes, which will follow on the initial shift of demand, as single chains, neglecting for the moment the successive ramifications which will occur at every link. Such a chain may either very soon lead to the other country or first run through a great many links at home. But whether any particular individual in the country will be affected will depend on whether he is a link in that particular chain, that is whether he has more or less immediately been serving the individuals whose income has first been affected, and not simply on whether he is in the same country or not.[36]

Hayek concludes that this disaggregated approach to balance-of-payments analysis reveals "how superficial and misleading the kind of argument is which runs in terms of the prices and the incomes of the country, as if they would necessarily move in unison or even in the same direction. It will be prices and incomes of particular industries which will be affected and the effects will not be essentially different from those which will follow any shifts of demand between different industries or localities."[37]

If fact, it is the unwarranted concentration upon aggregates and averages in conjunction with a quirk of statistical compilation that has prevented economists from grasping the simple truth that all prices in a given nation need not move in the same direction to equilibrate the balance of payments. As Hayek points out, it is "the purely accidental fact" that price levels are constructed for prices in a national area that leads to the mistaken belief "that in some sense all prices of a country could be said to move together relatively to prices in other countries." Needless to say, "[t]he fact that the averages of (more or less arbitrarily selected) groups of prices move differently in different countries does of course in no way prove that there is any tendency of the price structure of a country to move as a whole relatively to prices in other countries."[38]

There is a second aspect to Hayek's case against the use of terms like "inflation" and "deflation" to describe the effects of the international money flows that occur under the gold standard. This derives from the fact that, under the international gold standard, gold serves in effect as a "homogeneous international currency," and that, therefore, changes in the quantity of money in a particular nation have no more and no less significance than changes in the quantity of money in a particular city or even household. The reason is that each of these units, including the nation, does not form an independent "currency area" but is a constituent of the world currency area that employs gold as the general medium of exchange.

Barring a change in the world's supply of gold, a net transfer of money from one nation to another in the long run will only occur in response to a relative change in the aggregate demands for money between the two areas. But the same is true today of a net transfer of dollar balances from one region to another within the United States or dollar currency area. In the latter case, we would hardly refer, let us say, to the loss of dollars in New Jersey and the acquisition of these currency units by New York residents as constituting a monetary deflation and inflation respectively. Thus to assert that fluctuations in national stocks of money under the international gold standard constitute deflation or inflation is to confuse "redistributions of money between areas" that are components of a unified currency area with changes in "the quantity of money in a closed system."[39]

This point has been well illustrated by Lord Robbins:

> Consider for a moment certain possible movements within a closed economy where there is only one monetary system. Suppose that in part of this economy there take place changes which involve changes in the relative value of products or factor services rendered in the area— a discovery, for instance, of valuable mineral resources, a changed fashion in tourism, or (what sometimes happens after periods of wars or disorganization) an improvement in labor productivity in respect of articles in elastic demand. Clearly, in such circumstances, we should expect a rise in money incomes in that area and, insofar as some products were not cheapened by the original cause of the movement, a corresponding rise in their prices. Would we call this inflation? Well, of course, this is a semantic question; words can mean what you like, but I should have thought that to call a movement of this sort inflationary was decidedly inconvenient and confusing. You only have to carry the thing to its limit and consider the rise of prices and the accompanying rise of incomes of a single industry, due to any of the causes I have mentioned, to see how very odd that would be.
>
> Now exactly the same thing can occur in national areas which are parts of the world economy. If the demand for their product rises in comparison with the demand for the products of other areas, or if the volume of these products forthcoming in markets of elastic demand increases, then, in a regime of fixed exchange rates, the way in which the workers and owners of productive resources situated there can receive the increased share of world production which is awarded to them by the market is just this: that domestic incomes and prices of home products rise *pari passu*, and the increase of real incomes comes via increased power to buy import goods, goods with import ingredients, or various kinds of foreign services.... Movements of this sort therefore can be conceived in a world in which the movements of price levels in the world as a whole are not inflationary.[40]

In light of the foregoing considerations, Heilperin concludes that serious or "fundamental" balance-of-payments disequilibria, requiring large and broad-based adjustments in a nation's internal price structure, do not arise from the day-to-day operation of the gold standard, but from the attempts of government monetary authorities to frustrate such operation. In Heilperin's words, "[i]n a free economy the principal cause of a cumulative deficit in a country's international payments is to be found in inflation."[41] Deficits due to rising domestic prices caused by monetary inflation are in turn exacerbated by outflows of short-term funds and the discouragement of long-term capital investment by foreigners, as a result of widespread loss of confidence in the ability of the government to maintain convertibility of the domestic currency in the face of persistently cumulating deficits and gold outflows. Continued inflation under these circumstances leads to a breakdown of the gold standard and of exchange rate stability.

Writes Heilperin: "A sustained policy of inflation leads a gold-standard country to a cumulative loss of gold and finally to the abandonment of that system; then the national currency can freely depreciate. In a country whose currency is not convertible into gold, inflation leads to its continuous devaluation in terms of foreign currencies."[42]

Thus it is not adherence to the international gold standard that imposes the sacrifice of domestic price stability on a nation. To the contrary, it is the pursuit of inflationary monetary policies leading ultimately to the abolition of the gold standard which precipitates both internal and external instability in the form of an upward spiraling of domestic prices and a corresponding free fall of the national currency on the foreign exchange market. The operation of the gold standard, when correctly understood, therefore poses no dilemma between internal and external stability: "Under 'normal' [noninflationary] conditions there is no need to choose between stable prices and stable exchanges. Not only can both be stable at the same time, but it clearly follows...that they must be stable simultaneously, if equilibrium is to be preserved."[43]

But what of the "abnormal" case in which a relatively large domestic inflation has driven a government to repudiate its pledge to redeem the national currency in gold? Under these circumstances, doesn't the "currency stabilization" and restoration of the gold standard require (a possibly great and protracted) internal deflation of money and prices? The answer is "no"; all the monetary authorities need do in this situation is cease further inflation of the stock of money and then tie back onto gold at a devalued parity that approximately reflects the magnitude of the previous inflation.

This is the policy advocated by Heilperin: "There is one set of circumstances where a 'floating rate' is not merely acceptable but, indeed, necessary. It is when a currency got out of line with other currencies, due to major internal inflation, to external world market circumstances (including a severe depression in one of the major economic centres of the world), or to war, and a new parity for it must be found."[44]

This, in fact, was the course pursued by France under the Poincaré reforms of 1926–28 and then, again, when convertibility of the franc was reestablished in 1958. In neither case did France undergo a deflation and depression of economic activity. Jacques Rueff, who was significantly involved in the implementation of both sets of reforms, reports that, in 1926, "[t]he guiding idea was to single out the exchange rate which would entail no reduction in wages because of the price in francs it would set for foreign goods. The difficulties experienced by the English from 1925 to 1930 in attempting to maintain a rate which would have preserved foreign markets for British goods only by an unachievable reduction of wages demonstrates the wisdom of this last criterion."[45]

The causes and unfortunate consequences of the British decision to return to the gold standard in 1925 at a considerably overvalued parity have been well described by Heilperin:

> With a view to restoring London's former prestige and influence as financial centre, England returned to the gold standard at the pre-war parity, while the pound was in fact depreciated by 10 per cent. This imposed the necessity of deflation so as to reduce gold prices to a level on which British export industries would become again competitive in the world market. The deflation proved, however, extremely difficult to carry through on account of rigidities in the price structure and particularly in the level of wages. The pound remained an overvalued currency and the British export industries suffered severely. This particular maladjustment would not have come into existence had the pound been stabilized at a lower and economically more justified gold parity.... The dilemma "deflation versus devaluation" has made a great career in the course of the last depression. Its roots are perhaps to be found in the British experience of 1925–32.[46]

In short, the price of gold must be altered after an extended bout of fiat money inflation to ensure a smooth transition back to the gold standard. Once the gold standard is again normally operating, there is no further need to tamper with gold parities to guarantee monetary stability throughout the world currency area.

This brings us to the final objection to the international gold standard on the grounds of its alleged incompatibility with domestic macroeconomic stability. Granted that the normal operation of the gold standard secures tolerable long-run price stability in the world economy, is it not still the case that it facilitates the international transmission of random shocks or monetary policy errors originating in one nation? For example, a rise in prices generated by an abnormally expansionary monetary policy in a large nation will result in a balance-of-payments surplus and influx of gold for a nation pursuing a relatively noninflationary monetary policy. If it strictly adheres to the gold standard, the latter nation will be denied recourse to an "autonomous" or "independent" monetary policy designed to dampen the inflationary impact on domestic prices. Conversely, a contraction of economic activity abroad will generate a balance-of-payments deficit and loss of gold reserves for the nation in question, due to a falling off of demand for its products on depressed world markets. The resulting contraction of its money stock will create excess supply in the domestic goods market, thus depressing domestic prices, employment, and real income.

All this, we are told, can be avoided at very little cost by the simple instrumentality of a freely floating national fiat currency. Under this monetary regime, when expansionary pressure is exerted on a nation from abroad, the exchange rate will simply float upward, obviating the need for balance-of-payments adjustment via inflation of domestic money and prices. Contrariwise, foreign depressions will be stopped dead at the nation's borders by a painless depreciation of the exchange rate, which substitutes for the grinding shrinkage of money, prices, and economic activity imposed by the gold standard.

Heilperin raises two objections to this seemingly impregnable case for fluctuating exchange rates. First, he contends that the national monetary and economic independence that is promised is far from costless; it is, in fact, purchased at the price of the breakup of the world currency area secured by the international gold standard and of the loosening of the only effective anti-inflation restraint binding the hands of national monetary authorities.

In Heilperin's words, "[t]he real meaning of the gold standard...is that it allows the various currencies to be freely converted into one another and thus gives the best practical approximation to a world currency."[47] "Thus the international gold standard minimizes the disturbing effects which a plurality of national currencies can have upon international commercial and financial relations."[48] In addition, the position of gold "as the base of money and credit is the only way of insuring against wide fluctuations in the values of currencies.... And the sensitive response of the money supply to the flow of gold in and out of a country would be the most effective discipline on national economic policies."[49]

Now, Heilperin admits that there exists "an abstract possibility of monetary internationalism," that is, stable exchange rates and nondistorted trade and financial flows, under a regime of fluctuating exchange rates. However, the abstract model is not borne out by actual experience.[50] This is certainly the lesson to be drawn from the 1930s:

Policies of "insulation" tend to break up international economic relations. The early monetary "autonomists" thought in terms of stable price levels at home and fluctuating exchange rates between currencies. On paper such a scheme had its attractions; in practice it proved unacceptable even to the planistic governments. Exchange fluctuations incited speculation and led to crises of confidence; "flights of capital" ensued. The international chaos, following upon the break-up of the international monetary system, proved very favorable to the growth of "hot money." Governments faced with crises of confidence and capital flights found exchange control and restriction on foreign payments the easiest way out.... Instead of stable internal price levels and fluctuating exchange rates between currencies, the practice developed of "pegging" foreign exchange rates protected by exchange control and associated with internal inflations.[51]

Admittedly, the world of the 1930s represents an extraordinary case, as governments struggled to export their unemployment problems and to reflate their economies out of the depression. Nonetheless, with theoretical insight leavened by this historical experience, Heilperin in 1952 was able to foresee accurately the broad outlines of a world of fluctuating national fiat currencies.

According to Heilperin:

The freedom of action...which individual countries, large or small, have in the absence of an international monetary system makes it possible to have a large number of national inflations going on simultaneously, differing in intensity and sheltered by exchange controls and import restrictions adopted by the respective governments. These simultaneous and concurrent national inflations are a characteristic feature of a world of "independent" currency systems "insulated" from one another and "protected" by national "full employment" and "development" programmes.... In addition, habits of inflation become so widely accepted that inflation as a "way of life" comes to be regarded by many politicians and even economists as entirely rational and acceptable.[52]

Now I submit that the foregoing is a much more accurate forecast of the outcome of the post–Bretton Woods (or actually post–Smithsonian agreement) experiment with fluctuating fiat currencies than can be derived from the abstract model presented by contemporary monetarist proponents of freely floating exchange rates. According to the latter, fluctuating exchange rates would lead to a decline in protectionism, as governments soon learned that they no longer need worry about their nation's external payments position, which is quickly and automatically equilibrated by appropriate movements of the exchange rate. Moreover, we were advised that the world would attain a greater overall degree of

macroeconomic stability, since more sophisticated and prudent governments could now undertake "independent" monetary policies and would
no longer be locked into automatically importing the consequences of
errors and excesses in monetary policy committed by governments of
lesser intelligence and self-restraint.

While the monetarist scenario is admittedly one theoretically possible outcome of a regime of fluctuating exchange rates, it is certainly not
the scenario that unfolded in the past decade. In fact the monetarist
predictions come to grief precisely because they ignore (which Heilperin
does not) the sociological insight that governments are inherently inflationary institutions whose propensity to create money can only be
curbed in practice by the gold standard. Furthermore, in order to camou-
flage highly visible and unpopular consequences of monetary inflation,
such as depreciating exchange rates and higher import prices, governments can naturally be expected to resort to such expedients as pegging
exchange rates at overvalued levels and placing restrictions on international trade and investment.

Another feature of the current scene which the advocates of freely
floating exchange rates failed to anticipate is the magnitude of the speculative flows of short-term funds. These flows result from the uncertainty generated by the ever present prospect of potentially large and
sudden alterations in exchange rates, which is due, in turn, to volatile
expectations regarding relative changes in national rates of inflation.
This effect did not escape Heilperin, however, who concluded that
"international finance is certain to be disturbed by exchange fluctuations. The absence of stable exchanges is a deterrent to long-term foreign
lending—not the only one, it is true, but a very important one. And as
regards short-term financial transactions, exchange fluctuations and
their expectations are one of the most powerful incentives to speculation
and to 'flights of capital.' Whenever such financial disturbances happen,
exchange fluctuations will become large and cumulative."[53]

Besides facilitating inflations (and subsequent recessions) and pro-
moting political barriers against international trade and investment, fluctuating exchange rates thus reduce world income in two additional ways.
First, speculative activities on the foreign exchange market absorb scarce
resources that would otherwise be employed in productively serving
consumers' demands. And, second, the increased uncertainty associated
with international commercial and financial transactions reduces their
volume and creates distortions in their pattern from the point of view of
the optimal allocation of resources dictated by comparative
advantage.

Heilperin anticipates the well-known monetarist counterargument
that the foreign exchange market provides facilities for "hedging" against
exchange rate fluctuations by noting that "[i]n the long run, however,

such 'hedging' is of no avail. As regards current trade, this is a short-term transaction and therefore fairly immune to exchange fluctuations. But the international division of labor and the regional (and national) specialization of production is a long-run proposition."[54]

Not only is the attempted insulation of the national economy through a policy of fluctuating exchange rates exceedingly costly, but, Heilperin argues, it is a goal that can never be successfully achieved as long as the nation's residents are free to carry on any international economic relations whatever. Fluctuating exchange rates cannot ensure internal stability—although they may indeed stabilize some arbitrarily selected price index—because a country's internal price structure or actual pattern of relative prices is primarily determined by world market forces. Thus:

> The very *fact* of international trade ought to convey a warning to advocates of a choice [between internal and external stability]! Fluctuating exchanges *must* affect the formation of prices within any one country, and do so to an increasing degree as foreign trade plays a more important part in the economy of a country. Countries which are working with imported raw materials could hardly maintain stable internal prices when exchanges of the countries from which they import raw materials fall or rise. If advocates of internal stability, as opposed to international stability, would state their case in terms of the structure of prices and not in terms of average price levels, they would see at once that their case is very weak, unless of course, they go on to condemn the whole of foreign trade as a disturbing factor and proceed to advocate a policy of autarchy.[55]

As a proponent of the Austrian theory of the business cycle developed by Mises and Hayek, Heilperin emphasizes the key role of relative changes between the prices of capital goods and the prices of consumers' goods, which are wrought by monetary inflation, in precipitating business fluctuations.[56] But a system of fluctuating exchange rates does not interfere with the international transmission of changes in relative prices; it merely neutralizes the external forces acting upon a given nation's absolute level of prices. Indeed, the free market proponents of freely floating exchange rates tirelessly proclaim that one of the greatest virtues of their scheme is that it does not preclude the international changes in relative prices which are needed to induce a rearrangement of productive activities according to the ever changing dictates of comparative advantage.

This is precisely the reason, however, why Heilperin and the Austrians deny that fluctuating exchange rates can successfully insulate a nation from macroeconomic fluctuations generated abroad. For example, when the monetary authorities of a foreign nation of significant size inflate their national money supply, typically via the expansion of bank loans to business borrowers in their own nation, the prices of capital or "higher order" goods are bid up, not just in the inflating nation but throughout the world economy, since commodity markets are internationally integrated. The increase of prices of capital goods relative to the prices of consumer goods signals business firms in the relevant industries in all nations to expand the output of capital goods and contract the output of consumers' goods. The stimulus to production of capital goods will continue until the inflation is brought to a halt. At that time, a reverse movement of inflation-distorted relative prices occurs and business leaders finally realize that many of the long-term investments made in the capital goods industries during the inflationary boom are unprofitable and must be liquidated. The revelation of these malinvestments and misallocations of productive factors coincides with the onset of a worldwide recession or depression.

Internationally integrated capital markets provide a further mechanism for transmitting the business cycle from country to country. Thus the impulse to (artificially) lower interest rates on the money and capital markets of the country experiencing bank credit expansion will swiftly spread throughout the world economy, as domestic and foreign investors are induced by the developing interest rate differential to shift their funds to higher yielding investments abroad. In addition, foreign business firms will find it profitable to expand the sales of their securities in that market where security prices have begun to rise above world levels due to declining interest rates, while restricting their borrowings and security offerings on their respective domestic credit markets. Such equilibrating shifts in the supply of and demand for savings between national capital markets (actually submarkets) ensure that a strictly national bank credit inflation will tend to uniformly drive down interest rates throughout the world economy. This fall in interest rates will give further impetus to the worldwide boom in prices and production of capital goods, since lower interest rates promote an increase in the capital values of long-lived plant and equipment. On the other hand, when the inflating nation calls a halt to further creation of bank credit, an impulse to rising interest rates travels throughout international capital markets, precipitating a global collapse of the capital values of investment goods and the onset of recession.

As long as it engages in international trade, therefore, a country may undergo a boom-and-bust cycle with a perfectly "stable" national price level, protected by floating exchange rates, when there occur reversible changes in relative prices and interest rates in world commodity and capital markets, which are the result of an inflationary boom engineered by foreign monetary authorities. The alleged benefits of a system of fluctuating exchange rates, purchased at the substantial cost of the demolition of an international money, thus turn out to be only a mirage of macroeconomic theorizing.

Heilperin thus contends that "the view must be denounced according to which economic disturbances and fluctuations are an imported evil, against which a country can insulate itself through fluctuating exchange. The main body of the theory of business cycles is worked out on the assumption of a closed economy. International relations spread and synchronize economic fluctuations."[57]

While Heilperin does not specifically identify the process by which business fluctuations are internationally transmitted, as I have done above, he is the only Austrian business-cycle theorist to address the problem within the context of a world of open economies under a system of fluctuating exchange rates. And the broad conclusions of his investigation are clear-cut:

> Even in the absence of an international monetary system, however, inflation, albeit *primarily* a domestic phenomenon of individual countries, is far from being *exclusively* that. Even though various countries have "independent" monetary systems . . . inflation taking place in any one nation may have—and often does have—repercussions which go beyond that country's confines. This is especially true if the country experiencing inflation is an important economic unit. . . . An economically important country, if it experiences inflation, can generate inflation elsewhere. The same is, of course, true of deflations which follow upon the breakdown of an inflationary process. Thus, even in the absence of an international monetary system, important economic units can transmit the "virus" of inflation to other countries.[58]

Heilperin points to the U.S. inflation to finance the Korean War as an empirical illustration of his thesis:

> In the first place . . . we tend to draw towards the United States an excessive share of the raw materials supply [higher order or capital goods] of the Western world, thereby furthering the already-described inflationary tendencies. In the second place, this pyramiding of production for military needs upon production for undiminished civilian needs may inevitably lead to an overextension of our productive capacity in the capital goods field, which has particular relevance to the problem of the business cycle. Since the United States has become the world's "leader" in any major inflationary or deflationary movements . . . [a]n American inflation and overinvestment in American industry are not merely grave domestic problems, they are serious international problems as well.[59]

A Critical Summing Up

Although Heilperin's work provides invaluable insights into the theory and history of the gold standard, the case he makes for the desirability of such a standard is considerably weakened by his view of the origin and nature of money and monetary institutions. In a word, Heilperin is a "monetary constructivist," who believes that money is basically a tool that is deliberately designed to be of use in achieving the economic policy goals of the national government. This contrasts with the Mengerian or Austrian conception of money as an undesigned social institution that emerged spontaneously from free market economic processes and whose primary function is to coordinate the diverse and multitudinous plans of market participants.[60]

This issue is raised here not to detract from Heilperin's substantial contributions, but to illustrate how a basic, and today widely accepted, misconception about money's role in the market economy can have serious implications for policy espousal. This is a particularly timely issue since, as we shall see, Heilperin's error vitiates the most publicized of the recent proposals to reestablish the gold standard, namely the gold price rule advocated by Arthur Laffer, Jude Wanniski, Robert Mundell, and others.[61] Finally, Heilperin's work is singularly well suited as the focus for this critique, precisely because he is a fearless logician who explicitly and consistently pursues the implications of his analysis to their conclusion in policy advocacy.

As I have mentioned, Heilperin regards money as a deliberate construction of the politico-legal system. This is evident from his definition of a monetary standard: "a monetary standard is a commodity the price of which, in terms of the national monetary unit, is fixed by the monetary law of the country and held stable by the monetary authorities of that country."[62] This implies that the national monetary unit exists as a disembodied name prior to and independently of the commodity legally designated as the monetary standard, and, indeed, Heilperin repeatedly warns against confusing the two. For example, he writes: "The fact that currency can be converted on demand into some one commodity (say, gold) at a fixed price, does not make that currency a commodity. It is merely a currency based on a commodity standard."[63] Elsewhere he declares that "One cannot emphasize too often the fact that a gold-standard currency is a paper currency attached to gold (and sometimes convertible into gold); it is not a gold currency."[64] Unfortunately, Heilperin supplies only the vaguest hint concerning the historical process by which a full-bodied, market-chosen commodity money gets transformed into the politicized and dematerialized money of the classical gold standard.[65]

Heilperin recognizes that an important implication of this view is that the historical gold standard is itself the product of a government price-fixing scheme, pure and simple. In his words:

> The essential feature of [the gold standard]...is the fact of fixing the price of gold in terms of the national monetary unit and the maintenance of that price by the central bank or the treasury, according to the way in which the monetary system is organized. It will be observed that gold-standard currency is not gold currency but paper money administered in such a way to keep the price of gold stable.... [I]t will be observed that convertibility is a necessary feature of the system, since this is precisely the instrument by means of which the price of gold is stabilized. More than that: the obligation for the central bank to buy and to sell gold at a certain price is a more fundamental feature of the system than the long-run fixity of that price. A currency remains linked to gold as long as gold can be bought and sold in unlimited quantities at a price controlled by the monetary authorities—even should that price be changed by the competent authorities at a subsequent date.[66]

In fact Heilperin counts it as a liability of the classical gold standard that it fostered the belief that the price of gold in terms of the national currency was to remain permanently fixed and never to be used as a policy variable in remedying balance of payments disequilibria. Thus, he decries the fact that "[t]here was no consistent method, under the gold standard, of handling major balance-of-payments disturbances. Even though every country had the right to change the gold parity of its currency at will, this was not being done and there developed a widespread—but erroneous—impression that gold standard countries were pledged to the maintenance of the 'gold content' of their monetary unit under all circumstances. Yet, at times, changes in the economic conditions of a country make it very advisable to alter the foreign-exchange value of its currency by modifying its parity."[67]

As a creation of national sovereignties, whose monetary authorities must operate the system according to "rules of the game," the gold standard is therefore inherently "a managed currency system."[68] According to Heilperin, "Even the pre-war gold standard [before 1914] was, to some extent, a managed currency. It is true that the range of discretionary powers enjoyed by central bankers was limited and that the principles of administering the monetary system were very clear and simple, but the fact remains that the system was rather managed than automatic."[69]

A further implication of the assumption that the gold standard is a purposive creation of the political authorities is that there exist identifiable goals that the system was designed to attain. According to Heilperin, the primary purpose of the gold standard is to ensure international monetary equilibrium in a world in which "monetary policy is a prerogative of national authorities."[70] Thus: "What must be made quite clear is that the function of gold reserves is not to 'guarantee' the 'value' of bank notes, but to make it easier to maintain international monetary stability.... [T]he principal monetary function of gold is that of meeting deficits in international payments...."[71]

A second, though subsidiary, purpose of a gold-convertible currency is to limit the potential for monetary inflation: "By making it impossible for the monetary circulation to rise above a certain multiple of gold reserves held by the monetary authorities one limits the possibility for prices to rise and thus makes it easier for gold reserves to meet disequilibria in international payments."[72]

Accordingly, Heilperin contends that for a nation lacking international economic relations, there is absolutely no purpose to be served by the gold standard: "In an isolated community ('closed economy') there would be no point in establishing the gold standard except as a transitory system leading from an all-gold currency to a paper currency having no link with gold whatever."[73]

These considerations lead Heilperin to adopt the position that a gold standard featuring limited convertibility, such as the Ricardian gold bullion standard, is to be preferred to one in which the national currency is fully convertible. He argues that "it is quite in keeping with an international gold standard that convertibility should be limited in such a way as to discourage 'internal drains' of gold without obstructing international movements of the metal. This was achieved after the [first world] war by means of suppressing the convertibility of notes into coin while retaining the obligation for the central bank to buy and to sell gold in bars (the so-called 'gold bullion standard')."[74]

Heilperin's (qualified) defense of the Bretton Woods agreement against the criticisms of traditional advocates of a gold standard, such as Benjamin M. Anderson, Edwin W. Kemmerer, and Melchior Palyi,[75] can also be traced to his underlying view of the gold standard as a creation of national governments, which has as its primary purpose the equilibration of national balances of payments under reasonably stable exchange rates. The smooth operation of the international gold standard requires common observance of the rules of the game by the various independent national monetary authorities.[76] Such observance could be counted upon without explicit international agreement prior to 1914, due to the generally prevailing spirit of liberal internationalism.[77] After World War I, however, the international gold standard was never adequately reconstructed and subsequently collapsed, because the formal agreements needed to replace the spontaneous adherence to the unwritten rules of a liberal, internationalist monetary regime were never forthcoming. So, for

Heilperin, the Bretton Woods agreement represented at least a first small step toward securing the international cooperation necessary to facilitate the operation of the gold standard on a world scale.[78]

Thus, Heilperin argued: "the Bretton Woods plan [is]...the nearest approximation to the gold standard we can achieve in the present-day world, a world in crisis, in turmoil, in distress, a world of strong nationalism, sadly lacking in international confidence. The gold standard is a memory from the past, and—it may be hoped—a possibility for the future; but for the present, at least, it is not a practical plan."[79]

It is instructive to contrast Heilperin's position on the nature and usefulness of the international gold standard with that of Melchior Palyi, one of the traditionalist proponents of the gold standard who Heilperin opposed in the debate over Bretton Woods. According to Palyi, gold money was not a creation of national governments but an organic component of the world market economy: "The gold standard in the classical sense was part and parcel of an economic order. It was a keystone of the system of public law, social customs and institutions, called 'capitalism'...a system that rested on what appears in perspective as virtually unlimited freedom of consumer choice, business enterprise, and markets."[80]

It follows, therefore, that the gold standard was not an instrument to be used by the political authorities for their own ends but rather by the public to protect their persons, goods, and markets against the political authorities. Palyi contends that the gold standard

> was an essential instrument of economic freedom. It protected the individual against arbitrary measures of the government by offering a convenient hedge against "confiscatory" taxation, as well as against the depreciation or devaluation of the currency. It was an instrument of "mobility" within and beyond national borders. Above all, it raised a mighty barrier against authoritarian interferences with the economic process.... Authoritarians of all denominations had to keep their inflationary propensities under control and to refrain from excessive taxation in order to forestall the loss of people's confidence in the currency, the breakdown of the standard. The public purse had to be held tight.[81]

Moreover, since the gold standard was "no one's invention,"[82] it required only the most minimal cooperation among national monetary authorities. "It was an international 'game,' with only occasional and ad hoc 'central bank cooperation.' True, individual central banks helped each other in acute emergencies, but for short periods only."[83] Mainly, however, each nation had to refrain from monetary inflation and the gold standard would operate smoothly all around. Thus, "[n]o country could count on foreign aid for sustained indulgence in credit expansion. Each had to be amenable to monetary discipline, and to rely on the enlightened long-range self-interest of all participants in the 'game,' including the vested interests of note-issuing institutions in protecting their own solvency."[84]

Consequently, in Palyi's view, the Bretton Woods agreement was not a necessary precondition for the postwar reconstruction of the gold standard, but quite the opposite. It was a way of institutionalizing the currency devaluation that would inevitably result in the destruction of the international gold standard. For, contrary to Heilperin, Palyi did not consider changing the "price" of gold as a policy option to be utilized by the monetary authorities in the case of severe balance-of-payments difficulties. Rather, he saw devaluation as an inflationary political intervention aimed at evading the discipline of the gold standard. Thus, he argued that "[t]here is probably no more effective tool with which to inflate the monetary base on which the credit structure rests than tinkering with the currency's gold content."[85]

And it was on these grounds that Palyi intransigently opposed the international monetary scheme hatched at Bretton Woods, arguing that "deliberate devaluation became acceptable as an instrument of monetary policy.... In 1944 this novel 'instrument' of deceiving the creditors was 'legalized' in the Bretton Woods Agreement, if only for cases of 'fundamental disequilibrium'."[86]

The foregoing exercise of explicitly tracing out the links between a writer's basic conception of money and his monetary policy recommendations leads to two important conclusions.

The first is that a consistent case for a genuine gold standard, for a monetary system characterized by full and unconditional convertibility of all paper claims to gold so that the monetary unit is effectively a weight unit of gold,[87] must rest on the insight of Carl Menger and the Austrian school that the institution of money is an "organic" or a spontaneous outgrowth of the market economy.[88] As Heilperin's writings so clearly demonstrate, acceptance of the postulate that money is an artifact of government policymakers leads logically, if unwittingly, to the advocacy of monetary arrangements that, at best, bear only a nominal resemblance to the classical gold standard.

The second benefit of this discussion is that it permits us to identify the implicit premises of those current writers, connected with the supply-side movement, who argue in favor of the implementation of a new gold standard or even a new Bretton Woods. Like Heilperin, these writers advocate the central bank "fix" the price of gold, via purchases and sales of gold or even through open market operations. Now, as noted, this policy of constraining the monetary authority to adhere to a "price rule" in emitting fiat currency hardly qualifies as a gold standard in any historically meaningful sense of that term. More important, however, it is clear that those who favor this type of link between gold and the dollar share Heilperin's presupposition that gold is not the social medium of exchange that evolved to coordinate disparate plans in the marketplace but a useful political tool that is to be wielded by government planners to alter the spontaneous price-and-quantity outcomes of the free market in order to assure preconceived macrostatistical goals. In the case of the modern proponents of the gold price rule, the goal is the stability of some statistical price index for which the gold price is considered a good proxy.

These insights should help prevent any confusion between the positions of traditional advocates of a gold standard and those who have recently declared for a new gold standard.

Notes

1. Details regarding Heilperin's life and career are difficult to come by. I have pieced together the following biographical sketch mainly from the dust jackets of his books. *The 1964 Handbook of the American Economic Association* also provided some useful information. Michael Angelo Heilperin was born May 6, 1909 in Warsaw, Poland. He received both his undergraduate degree and his doctorate in economics from the University of Geneva, in 1929 and 1931 respectively. He also pursued graduate studies at the London School of Economics and Cambridge University. From 1935 to 1938, he was an assistant professor on the faculty of the Graduate Institute of International Studies in Geneva. In the 1930s, he also taught at a number of academic institutions in the United States, including Bryn Mawr College in Pennsylvania and the University of California at Berkeley. In 1941 he was appointed associate professor of economics at Hamilton College in New York, a position he resigned in December 1945. He returned to the Graduate Institute in Geneva in 1953, where he served as professor of international economics until 1964. During this period he also served as an associate editor and West European correspondent of *Fortune Magazine*. From 1964 to 1966 he was also a member of the magazine's board of editors. Heilperin held a visiting professorship in international finance at the University of Southern California in 1968. I was unable to track down any other biographical information on him after this date.

Heilperin published books and articles in three languages: Polish, French, and English. His works in French include his doctoral dissertation, completed in 1931, *Le Probleme Monetaire D'Apres-Guerre et la Solution en Pologne, en Autriche et en Tchecosloquie*, and a book, *Monnaie, Credit, et Transfert* (Paris, 1932). Heilperin's major works in English comprise the following books and monographs: Michael A. Heilperin, *International Monetary Economics* (London: Longmans, Green, 1939); *International Monetary Reconstruction: The Bretton Woods Agreements* (New York: American Enterprise Association, 1945); *The Trade of Nations* (New York: Alfred A. Knopf, 1947); *Studies in Economic Nationalism* (Geneva: Librairie E. Droz, 1960); and *Aspects of the Pathology of Money: Monetary Essays from Four Decades* (London: Michael Joseph Limited,

1968). The only article I was able to locate in an English language professional journal, aside from those collected in the last-named book, is Michael A. Heilperin, "Economics of Banking Reform," *Political Science Quarterly 50* (September 1935):359–76.

2. For example, Heilperin was a member of the prestigious "Bellagio group" of thirty-two academic economists brought together in 1964 by the late Fritz Machlup to consider questions of monetary reform. He was one of only two members of the group (Jacques Rueff was the other) to recommend a return to the classical gold standard, at a substantially increased price of gold. See International Finance Section, *International Monetary Arrangements: The Problem of Choice—Report on the Deliberations of an International Study Group of 32 Economists* (Princeton, N.J.: Princeton University, 1964), especially pp. 115–16 for Heilperin's dissent from the consensus view.

3. Rueff's critique can be found in Jacques Rueff, *The Age of Inflation,* translated by A.H. Meeus and F.G. Clarke (Chicago: Henry Regnery, 1964); *Balance of Payments: Proposals for the Resolution of the Most Pressing World Economic Problem of Our Time,* translated by Jean Clement (New York: Macmillan, 1967); *The Monetary Sin of the West,* translated by Roger Glemet (New York: Macmillan, 1972).

4. See, for example, many of the essays in Jack Kemp and Robert Mundell, eds., *A Monetary Agenda for World Growth* (Boston: Quantum, 1983).

5. See the criticisms of the various post-Keynesian approaches in Harry G. Johnson, "The Monetary Approach to the Balance of Payments: A Nontechnical Guide," *Journal of International Economics 7* (August 1977):251–68; and "Money and the Balance of Payments," *Banca Nazionale Del Lavoro Quarterly Review* (March 1976), pp. 3–18.

6. Heilperin, *International Monetary Economics,* p. 145.

7. Ibid., p. 7.

8. Ibid., p. 152.

9. Ibid., p. 154.

10. The curious absence of explicit reference to the demand for money mars all of Heilperin's work on international monetary economics. This is even more curious, given that Heilperin, by his own admission, worked "for three years in almost daily contact with Professor Ludwig von Mises," at the time (1935–38) the foremost Continental exponent of the cash-balance approach to the demand for money.

11. Heilperin, *International Monetary Economics,* pp. 155–56.

12. Ibid., p. 163.

13. Ibid., p. 148.

14. Ibid., pp. 163–64.

15. Ibid., p. 164.

16. Ibid., p. 192.

17. Heilperin, *Pathology of Money,* p. 257.

18. Alvin H. Hansen, *Monetary Theory and Fiscal Policy* (New York: McGraw-Hill, 1949), pp. 212–13.

19. Heilperin, *Pathology of Money,* p. 235.

20. Ibid., pp. 206–07.

21. On the genesis and destruction of the gold exchange standard in the 1920s, see Heilperin, *Pathology of Money*, pp. 173–75; and Murray N. Rothbard, *The Mystery of Banking* (New York: Richardson and Snyder, 1983), pp. 245–47.

22. Heilperin, *International Monetary Economics*, p. 213.

23. Ibid.

24. Ibid., p. 217.

25. Heilperin, *Pathology of Money*, pp. 270, 284.

26. Heilperin, *International Monetary Economics*, pp. 190–92.

27. Heilperin, *Pathology of Money*, p. 273.

28. Ibid., pp. 254–55.

29. For an overview of the Bretton Woods system, see Rothbard, *The Mystery of Banking*, pp. 251–54.

30. On the nature of "pattern prediction" in the social sciences, see F.A. Hayek, *Studies in Philosophy, Politics and Economics* (New York: Simon and Schuster, 1969), pp. 22–42.

31. J.M. Keynes, *A Tract on Monetary Reform* (London, 1923), pp. 154–55.

32. Heilperin, *International Monetary Economics*, p. 13.

33. Ibid., pp. 267–68.

34. Ibid., p. 169.

35. Ibid.

36. F.A. Hayek, *Monetary Nationalism and International Stability* (New York: August M. Kelley, 1964), pp. 21–22. Reprinted with permission.

37. Ibid., p. 23.

38. Ibid., p. 45.

39. Ibid., p. 24.

40. Lord Robbins, "Inflation: An International Problem" in Randall Hinshaw, ed., *Inflation as a Global Problem* (Baltimore: Johns Hopkins University Press, 1972), pp. 16–17. Also see Lionel Robbins, *Economic Planning and International Order* (London: Macmillan, 1937), pp. 281–83.

41. Heilperin, *International Monetary Economics*, p. 123.

42. Ibid.

43. Ibid., pp. 169–70.

44. Heilperin, *Pathology of Money*, p. 228.

45. Rueff, *The Age of Inflation*, pp. 80–81. For a detailed description of the Poincaré reforms, see Benjamin M. Anderson, *Economics and the Public Welfare: A Financial and Economic History of the United States, 1914–1946* (Indianapolis: Liberty Press, 1979), pp. 164–70.

46. Heilperin, *Pathology of Money*, pp. 89–90.

47. Heilperin, *International Monetary Economics*, p. x.

48. Ibid., pp. 179–80.

49. Heilperin, *Pathology of Money*, p. 270.

50. Heilperin, *International Monetary Economics*, pp. 220–21.

51. Heilperin, *Pathology of Money*, pp. 169–70.

52. Ibid., p. 170.

53. Ibid., pp. 68–69.

54. Heilperin, *Trade of Nations*, p. 50. Reprinted with permission.

55. Heilperin, *International Monetary Economics*, p. 12.

56. For a sympathetic discussion of the Austrian theory of the business cycle, see especially Heilperin, *Pathology of Money*, pp. 153–62. Also see Heilperin, *International Monetary Economics*, pp. 91–94.

57. Ibid., p. 71.

58. Ibid., p. 164. Unfortunately, nowhere does Heilperin provide a more detailed description of the mechanism by which inflation is transmitted internationally under fluctuating exchange rates.

59. Ibid., p. 177.

60. For a comparison of these two approaches to money, see Joseph T. Salerno "Gold Standards: True and False," *The Cato Journal* 3 (Spring 1983): 261–67.

61. For a review and critique of this type of proposal from a Mengerian perspective, see ibid., pp. 258–61. Also see Salerno, *The Gold Standard: An Analysis of Some Recent Proposals*, Policy Analysis Series (Washington, D.C.: The Cato Institute, 1982).

62. Heilperin, *International Monetary Economics*, pp. 126–27.

63. Ibid., p. 16.

64. Ibid., p. 25, fn. 2.

65. Ibid., pp. 16–17, 176.

66. Ibid., pp. 176–77.

67. Heilperin, *Trade of Nations*, pp. 59–60. Reprinted with permission.

68. Heilperin, *International Monetary Economics*, p. 178, fn. 1.

69. Heilperin, *Pathology of Money*, p. 83. Heilperin even goes so far as to deny that a 100 percent gold standard or "simple specie currency" can operate automatically. In a world of international financial transactions, political management is necessary to implement the appropriate discount-rate policy in the face of balance-of-payments disequilibria (Heilperin, *International Monetary Economics*, pp. 152–53, 156). Without engaging in a detailed critique of this view, suffice it to say that Heilperin here ignores the important insight of Hayek that "with a homogeneous international currency [e.g., gold] there is apparently no reason why an outflow of money from one area and an inflow into another should necessarily cause a rise in the rate of interest in the first area and a fall in the second" (Hayek, *Monetary Nationalism*, p. 24).

70. Heilperin, *International Monetary Economics*, p. 95.

71. Ibid., pp. 181–85.

72. Ibid., p. 182.

73. Ibid., p. 178.

74. Ibid., p. 185. Also see Heilperin, *International Monetary Reconstruction*, p. 10.

75. Heilperin, *International Monetary Reconstruction*, pp. 79–80.

76. For an enumeration of the "rules," see ibid., pp. 10–11.

77. Ibid., p. 8.

78. Ibid., pp. 11–14; also Heilperin, *Trade of Nations*, pp. 144–57.

79. Heilperin, *International Monetary Reconstruction*, p. 80.

80. Melchior Palyi, *The Twilight of Gold 1914–1936: Myths and Realities* (Chicago: Henry Regnery, 1972), p. 5.

81. Ibid.

82. Ibid., p. 14.

83. Ibid., p. 11.

84. Ibid.

85. Melchior Palyi, *An Inflation Primer* (Chicago: Henry Regnery, 1961), p. 60.

86. Idem., *Twilight of Gold*, p. 281.

87. Salerno, *Gold Standards: True and False*, pp. 250–58. For a selected bibliography of works detailing the nature and operation of a pure commodity money, see p. 251, fn. 32 of the same work.

88. See ibid., pp. 261–67 for references to the relevant literature on this approach.

6
Free Banking and the Gold Standard

Lawrence H. White

T he conjunction of "free banking" with "the gold standard" in the title of this chapter suggests to me two questions: Is free banking necessary to a successful gold standard? And, conversely, is a gold standard necessary to a successful free banking system? My aim in what follows will be to see how much of a natural affinity can be found between the principles of the gold standard and the principles of a freely competitive monetary order, or to put it metaphorically, to see whether gold and free banking are really warp and woof of the fabric of a successful monetary system.

Focusing the chapter in this way admittedly may leave it with little to say to those who find neither free currency competition nor commodity money attractive or interesting. Its concerns will likely seem idle to those who find the current national systems of banking regulation *cum* fiat money part of the best of all possible worlds. There is encouraging evidence, however, that serious interest in alternative monetary systems, particularly the gold standard and various proposals for a laissez-faire approach to money, is on the rise both within academic circles and among participants in political affairs.

The Criteria for Monetary Success

Posing the question of how essential a free banking system is to the successful working of a gold-based monetary order obviously raises another question: What are the proper criteria for success in a monetary system? The answer to this second question is not obvious. Nor is it obvious by what method an economist can best go about developing an answer, if there is one. One approach that seems clearly inadequate is worth mentioning and criticizing because it is so popular: the method of sheer presumption. Too often economic analysts begin with what Gerald P. O'Driscoll, Jr., has aptly characterized as "a long 'laundry list' of macroeconomic goals to be achieved by a monetary standard."[1] The desirability of these goals is usually taken for granted by those who propose them. Worse, it is assumed without a second thought that the way to achieve a desirable monetary system is to use the political means to create institutions that can be programmed to generate the behavior in macroeconomic aggregates called for by the goals. That is, monetary institutions are viewed in purely macroinstrumental terms. They are tools that government policymakers may design or redesign, and the relative goodness of various institutional arrangements is to be judged solely by comparing the various statistical time series they generate. A "desirable" monetary system, on this view, is one that produces the outcomes presumed desirable by the analyst.

One alternative to the macroinstrumental approach for judging monetary systems is what we might call the microsovereignty (for "microeconomic" and "individual sovereignty") approach. It asks: How well does a particular system serve the interests of the individuals who use money, as those individuals themselves see their interests? Does it leave individuals desiring feasible alternative arrangements, yet block them from making the changes they desire? "Feasible" in this context means not just technologically feasible, but potentially achieving consent from all those traders whose participation is desired. The question, in more technical terms, is whether a monetary system leaves Pareto improvements uncaptured.

The microsovereignty approach is, of course, the approach most economists take to the question of the successfulness of arrangements for supplying virtually every good other than money. A "monetary system" is simply a set of institutions for supplying the economic good we call "money." No proper economist, speaking as an economist, would presume to judge the goodness of the current American playing card (or, for that matter, baseball card) system by contrasting its characteristics to a list of characteristics he thought desirable. None would fault the system for the possible unpredictability of the purchasing power or relative price of cards from year to year, or for the possible nonuniformity of cards from producer to producer. A proper economist would instead ask whether there existed any reason to suppose that card users were not getting the kinds of cards they wanted (that is, any kinds for which they were willing to pay cost-covering prices). He would not try to second guess consumers' preferences.

Why is money treated differently? It is probably because few economists are accustomed to thinking of money as a private good. Government provision of money has come to be taken for granted, especially so in this century of government fiat monies. *Given* the institution of state-issued fiat money, there clearly must be some definite government policy for regulating the quantity issued. *Given* the inescapability of monetary policy under a fiat regime, government clearly needs expert opinion regarding the desirable goals to be pursued by monetary policy and the technical means to pursue those goals effectively. Unlike a private firm producing playing cards in a competitive environment, a government producing money is not automatically guided by the profit-and-loss system toward meeting consumer wants. Government monetary authorities have no bottom line for which they are accountable. That of course is a major part of the explanation for their poor performance (poor by almost anyone's standards) over the past decades.

The possibility of free banking, if it means nothing else, means that government provision of money ought *not* be taken for granted. The fact that monetary policy becomes necessary when government produces money is no more an argument for treating money differently than other goods than is the fact that a playing card policy becomes necessary when government produces cards. The provision of all forms of money, like the provision of cards, can be left to the marketplace. If the microsovereignty approach is respected, then to argue that either good ought to be brought within the province of government requires one to make a case that free market provision leaves some subset of individuals frustrated in attempts to reach mutually preferred arrangements. This case must rely on more than just sheer presumption regarding the content of consumer preferences. It is one thing to attribute concrete preferences to consumers (for example, risk-averse preferences for low variance in aggregate nominal income[2]) for the sake of particular modeling exercises, although the value of such exercises is questionable, especially when individual preference functions are defined over economywide aggregates that no individual confronts directly. It is quite another thing to claim policy relevance for these models on the implicit assumption that real world consumers have the stipulated preferences. Some evidence of this ought to be provided, namely by reference to the preferences actually demonstrated by money users.

The gold standard in particular is often evaluated on the basis of the behavior of price indexes during the era of the classical gold standard. It is sometimes suggested that the successfulness of gold hinges on whether it produces relative stability or predictability in the purchasing power of money (which operationally means zero mean or low variance in the first differences of a price index). On the microsovereignty approach these would be among the proper criteria only if they were among the criteria money users themselves consulted in choosing among monetary standards.[3]

Certainly advocates of the gold standard need not view it purely in macroinstrumental terms as a device for producing approximate price-level stability. It is likely that few do view it in such a way. For one, there are alternative routes to price level stability, namely through various quantity-rule or price-index-rule devices for manipulation of the quantity of fiat money, that do not command much enthusiasm among those who value a gold coin standard. From the perspective that takes departures from the gold coin (specie) standard to be compromises of the gold standard ideal, the enthusiasm shown by some supply siders for a fiat money "price rule" looks more like a variant of (early) monetarism than like a wing of the traditional gold standard camp. The same applies to Fisherian "compensated dollar" schemes with or without gold trappings.[4] Second, the "dishonesty" of fiat money criticized by gold's partisans seems to be not so much its purchasing-power behavior as its potential for inflationary finance—that is, for covert taxation through expansion of the monetary base. Cash balances are taxed even under a fiat money policy that stabilizes the price level, namely by the difference between zero and the rate of appreciation of purchasing power that would be generated by fixing of the monetary base. This corresponds to the rate of base growth necessary to offset secular growth in real demand for base money. In historical experience, of course, inflationary finance has been much greater.

The following statement by Phillip Cagan, though it shows a greater effort to understand the progold position than other monetarists have made, nonetheless misinterprets the position of many in the gold camp:

> Stripped of its rhetoric, however, the position of the gold advocates is really a plea for a stable purchasing power of money, with as close to a guarantee of stability as one can obtain in this uncertain world. There is no logical basis for their opposition to any monetary system that provides a reasonable promise of a stable value of the currency. Why then do advocates of gold not support monetarism which shares the same goal?
>
> As far as I can see, the opposition is not over principle but rather over technique.[5]

There is every reason for gold standard advocates who personally value stability in the purchasing power of money indeed to support monetarism (that is, slow and steady growth in the money supply) in the sense of viewing it as preferable, within the context of a fiat money regime, to the sort of discretionary policy seen in the last decade. But again, price level stability is not, or need not be, the point of advocating a gold-based monetary system. The point may instead be minimization of avoidable interferences with provision of the types of money individuals desire to use. It is certainly possible to believe, based on the historical record, that gold and gold-redeemable instruments came to assume a monetary role precisely because they were the kinds of money people wanted to use. On this view the forced transition to fiat money was a contravention of individual sovereignty that ought to be reversed.

Free Banking and Individual Sovereignty

If the rationale for a gold standard lies in a microeconomic or individual sovereignty approach, then free banking clearly *is* necessary for the success of the system. Individual sovereignty in economic affairs amounts to the freedom of potential buyers and sellers to make their own bargains, unimpeded by third-party impositions or barriers.[6] It amounts, in other words, to free trade. A system of free banking entails free trade in the market for "inside" money (bank demand liabilities), particularly for bank notes. No legislative barriers are placed in the way of exchanges of bank notes and demand deposits between potential issuers and money users. Individuals are free to accept or reject the liabilities of particular banks as they see fit. Banks are free to pursue whatever policies they find advantageous in the issuing of liabilities and the holding of asset portfolios, subject only to the general legal prohibition against fraud or breach of contract.[7]

Bank demand liabilities under any monetary standard constitute sight claims to the economy's most basic money. Under a gold coin standard the most basic form of money is by definition coined precious metal or specie. Mintage services can be performed exclusively by competing private firms, and the ethic of free trade would suggest that they ought to be provided competitively rather than by government monopoly. Only under open competition are there market forces tending to ensure that consumers get coins having the attributes they demand, for example having the denominations (sizes) they find most convenient.[8] This question is independent, however, of the operation of the bank system.

Claims to specie issued by banks serve as money when transactors generally accept payments in the form of transfers of claims which they in turn transfer in payments to others. Titles to specie can then change hands without any specie physically moving. Historically bankers and their customers early discovered mutual advantage in the service of transferring deposit balances by book entries, sparing the need for making cumbersome withdrawals, transfers, and redeposits of gold. The personal check emerged as a means of signaling banks to perform such transfers. Later the bank note, payable to the bearer on demand, emerged as a means for transferring claims to specie without the involvement of the bank.[9] For particular purposes one or the other form of redeemable claim on bank specie is more convenient to use than actual specie. The ability of these claims to function as money—their general acceptability as means of payment—of course depends on their being regarded as actually redeemable for basic money at par on demand.[10] This feature fixes the exchange value of notes and demand deposits equal to that of the specie to which they are claims, enabling them to serve as substitutes for coin.

Under free banking individuals may choose among the notes of a plurality of private issuers. They are not limited to using the notes of a privileged central bank. Monopolization of note issue is a defining characteristic of central banking, and a characteristic that has always emerged from legislative intervention. There is no evidence of a tendency toward natural monopoly in the issue of bank notes.[11] Open competition in issue ensures that banks will provide notes with the characteristics note holders demand. The quality dimensions along which notes may differ include ease of redemption, reputability of issuer (this is a combination of trustworthiness and renown), and proof against counterfeiting. All of these will affect a note's most important characteristic, its ability to circulate. Competition among bank note issuers is in many respects similar to the competition we see today among issuers of credit cards and traveler's checks, as well as being similar to competition among banks for checking account customers.[12] Respect for microeconomic criteria and individual sovereignty requires that government not limit consumers' choices by interfering with competition among potential bank note issuers.

One argument sometimes made against competitive issue of bank notes (and which presumably also could be made against competitive issue of checking accounts, traveler's checks, and credit cards, though it rarely is) runs the following way: The reason people use money is to lower the information or transactions costs of accomplishing desired trades. Dealing with numerous brands of hand-to-hand currency implies bearing high information or transactions costs. Suppressing the number of issuers therefore improves economic welfare. I have elsewhere offered the rebuttal that this argument amounts to the paternalistic view that too much choice makes life difficult for people and should be eliminated by the government choosing for them; if valid in the case of bank notes, this argument would be valid against brand proliferation in any industry.[13] Here I wish to elaborate on that rebuttal. Consider an initial situation with only a single brand of bank notes. What is the case against allowing a second brand? Individuals (for example, shopkeepers) who do not wish to be bothered with the new brand can refuse to deal with it. If they do choose to deal with it (accept it), presumably they consider the information and transactions costs worth bearing in light of the benefits they expect. If the costs are generally considered not worth bearing, the market will not support a second brand. This holds for $n + 1$ brands as well as for two. The rationale of open competition among multiple brands of bank notes (as among brands of anything else) is the freedom to discover which brands and how many brands best suit consumer preferences. Central bank monopoly eliminates the chance for individuals to accept other brands of notes even when the benefit exceeds the cost.

Free Banking and Fractional Reserves

Discussion of free banking usually focuses on the liability side of banks' balance sheets, particularly on the freedom to issue bank notes. But freedom on the asset side is also controversial. The alternative assets banks on a gold standard choose among, when permitted, can be divided most simply into two categories: specie reserves and interest-earning assets such as loans and securities. A bank holds specie reserves to honor its contractual obligation to redeem on demand its notes and deposits. The size of the reserve it chooses reflects its perception of the risk of sudden redemption outflows. The bank holds interest-earning assets having varying degrees of ready marketability, the readiest serving as a "secondary reserve" that can be sold for gold to replenish the specie reserve on short notice.

Each category of assets has been historically subjected to government regulation. Restrictions on earning asset choices were part and parcel of so-called free banking legislation enacted by midnineteenth-century American states. Banks issuing notes were required to own, and to place in the possession of state regulators, certain types of assets, most notably state government bonds. Restrictions on reserve-holding choices, namely "reserve requirements," were imposed by several states before the Civil War. They have been part of federal regulation since the National Bank Act of 1863.[14] Both categories of asset regulation prevent consumers from freely choosing among banks with alternative portfolio policies and hence with alternative risk–return characteristics. They prevent banks from achieving desired risk–return performance most efficiently. The function of banknotes as hand-to-hand currency suggests that consumers will prefer the notes of issuers who present close to zero illiquidity and insolvency risk.[15] It also suggests that bank notes will generally be non–interest-bearing. The forces of competitive selection shaping bank asset portfolios will then focus primarily on the methods of producing consumer confidence in bank notes and deposits (exemplary past redemption performance, which depends on adequate reserves, being the chief method) and on the rates of return paid on deposits (these rates depend on bank holdings of interest-bearing assets). Under competitive conditions banks are compelled to act in compliance with consumer preferences in balancing the benefits of additional specie reserves (lesser chance of illiquidity) against the alternative benefit of additional interest-bearing assets (higher returns on deposits).

Some gold standard advocates, most notably Murray N. Rothbard, have argued for 100 percent reserve requirements against demand deposits and bank notes. Rothbard urges this position not as a paternalistic intervention into the market for inside money, but on the grounds that the holding of less than 100 percent reserves against demand liabilities is per se fraudulent. This argument is more jurisprudential than economic. He has recently written: "It should be clear that modern fractional reserve banking is a shell game, a Ponzi scheme, a fraud in which false warehouse receipts are issued and circulate as equivalent to the cash supposedly represented by the receipts." And in rebuttal to the argument that a banker hardly needs 100 percent reserves in order to meet all the redemption demands that will in fact confront him at any one time, he writes: "But holders of warehouse receipts to money emphatically *do have*...a claim, even in modern banking law, to their own property any time they choose to redeem it. But the legal claims issued by the bank must then be fraudulent, since the bank could not possibly meet them all."[16] Rothbard's view that bank notes are the legal equivalent of warehouse receipts is based on what he thinks legal practice *ought* to be, not on the interpretation courts have actually made of the contractual obligations incurred by the issuers of bank notes.[17]

It is difficult to see why an analyst committed to the ethic of individual sovereignty, as Rothbard elsewhere clearly is, would wish to prevent banks and their customers from making whatever sorts of contractual arrangements are mutually agreeable. The British Court decisions cited and criticized by Rothbard, to the effect that bank notes do not contractually bind their issuers to holding 100 percent reserves, seem eminently reasonable given the inscription actually found on the face of a typical British bank note: The Bank of XYZ "promise to pay the bearer on demand one pound sterling."[18] There is no promise made about reserve-holding behavior. There is nothing to indicate that the note constitutes a warehouse receipt or establishes a bailment contract. But ought it do so? On an individual sovereignty approach that depends on the contractual arrangement, a bank and its customer mutually desire. Nothing in a free banking system prevents an individual who desires 100 percent reserve banking from explicitly contracting for it. In historical fact safety deposit boxes have commonly been offered by banks for those who wish their money held as a bailment, who wish, in other words, to retain unconditional title to it. It would be silly to suggest that bank notes and demand deposits gained acceptance historically only when their holders were fraudulently misled by the misrepresentation of bank demand liabilities as unconditional warehouse receipts. It is in fact evident that most individuals will voluntarily accept nonbailment bank notes and demand deposits.

On a title-transfer view of contracts a bank note payable to the bearer on demand, with no stipulation of the reserves to be held, constitutes a *conditional* title to bank-held specie, conditional on presentation for redemption.[19] In a title-transfer regime prevention of breach of contract by banks issuing such notes requires only that any obligation to redeem on demand be satisfied for all customers who actually present notes and deposits for redemption. Fractional reserves do not constitute breach of contract. A bank furthermore may, consistent with title transfer, insert a clause into note and deposit contracts reserving to itself the option of delaying redemption. Historically the Scottish banks did this for notes before the practice was outlawed, and recent American NOW checking accounts have incorporated such a feature.[20] Such option clauses mean that a sudden redemption outflow from a bank can be headed off without breach of contract. In practice an issuer will not likely exercise the option to defer redemption, except in an emergency, because an expectation by the public that the option will be used would impair the circulability of the issuer's notes and hence would reduce the demand to hold those notes.

Free Banking and Macroeconomic Performance

In addition to the argument on microsovereignty grounds there is a case for free banking to be made on macroinstrumental grounds: The aggregate performance of an economy on a gold standard is likely to be better under free banking than under central banking. A large body of theoretical and historical work in economics identifies money supply errors as a significant source of business cycle disturbances.[21] The advantage of free banking is that a plurality of issuers minimizes the chances for large-scale errors in the money supply. One reason is readily apparent: No single issuer controls a large share of the circulation. Equally important, the plurality of issuers brings with it, in the form of the interbank clearinghouse for bank notes (and checks), an automatic mechanism for preventing major money supply errors by any single bank. The clearinghouse gives each issuer both the information to detect, and the incentive to correct promptly, any deviation of the quantity of inside money it supplies from the quantity of its inside money that the public desires to hold. This process of negative feedback is absent from a central banking system, where the supply of bank notes is monoplized and the liabilities of the central bank are held as reserves by commercial banks. Only with free banking is the operation of the gold standard fully self-regulating.

The contrast between free banking and central banking with regard to the mechanisms regulating the money stock can be spelled out here in somewhat greater detail.[22] The public's demand to hold the demand liabilities (notes or demand deposits) of any particular bank is a definitely limited magnitude (in nominal as well as real terms given that the purchasing power of notes and demand deposits is fixed by their redeemability for specie). Suppose a single bank in a multi-issuer system issues too many notes or deposits, "too many" being more than the public desires to hold. People who find themselves holding excess notes or deposits will get rid of them largely by depositing them in checking or savings accounts at their own banks, or by spending them away to persons who will deposit them. Given that our single bank is relatively small, all but a small fraction of the excess notes or deposits will wind up as deposits in rival banks. The rival banks that accept these deposits will quickly turn around and demand redemption of the first bank's liabilities through the interbank clearing system. The overexpansive bank will discover that its specie reserves are draining away, a situation it cannot let persist. Reserve losses signal to the bank the need to correct its course to prevent complete illiquidity. The negative feedback is rapid enough that any disturbance to the credit market or aggregate spending will likely be quite minor.

A central bank, by contrast, faces no rival for the circulation of its notes. Both its notes and its demand deposits may serve as reserves for commerical banks, displacing specie from that role. Hence an overexpansion of central bank liabilities, supposing one to occur, will not find its way into the clearing mechanism and thereby rapidly reveal its presence. Instead commercial banks that come to hold extra central bank liabilities will be impelled by their swollen reserves to expand their own liabilities. The resulting overexpansion of the entire system will be revealed only through a relatively slow and drawn-out process. An excess stock of money stimulates greater spending as individuals adjust their wealth portfolios. This leads to an "adverse" balance of trade with other nations, that is, an excess of imports over exports, both directly as the excess stock of money prompts greater spending on imports as well as on domestic goods, and indirectly as increased spending on domestic goods bids up their prices and makes imports more attractive. The excess of imports over exports must be paid in international currency, namely gold. Settlement of the balance then drains gold from the central bank's vault. The signal to reverse its course finally appears to the central bank.

But in the meantime the economy may have been driven through an artificial credit boom of major proportions which must be painfully reversed when the central bank contracts credit to stanch its reserve losses.

Even under a gold standard, then, a central bank may have sufficient leeway to issue sharp monetary shocks and thereby to generate severe business cycles. Much modern historical work remains to be done in exploring the applicability of this theory to business cycles actually experienced, particularly in Britain under the gold standard managed by the Bank of England after 1821 and in America under the Second Bank of the United States. There is no question that many sophisticated contemporary observers of the Bank of England under the classical gold standard blamed it for creating or aggravating business cycles through improper issuing policies. It is for this reason that the program of the well-known currency school called for restriction of the Bank of England's discretionary power of issuing notes. Such a restriction was embodied in Peel's Bank Charter Act of 1844. The free banking school of the same era argued more per ceptively and radically for an end to the legal privileges that bestowed on the Bank of England its central banking powers.[23] In the United States the Jacksonian case against the Second Bank of the United States, providing the rationale for the veto of its recharter in 1832, rested in part on the argument that its mismanagement of the currency had sent the economy through boom-and-bust cycles.[24]

The policy of free banking gained Ludwig von Mises' endorsement as an essential barrier against the experience of business fluctuations driven by overexpansionary central bank policies. Wrote Mises:

> Free banking is the only method available for the prevention of the dangers inherent in credit expansion. It would, it is true, not hinder a slow credit expansion, kept within very narrow limits, on the part of cautious banks which provide the public with all information required about their financial status. But under free banking it would have been impossible for credit expansion with all its inevitable consequences to have developed into a regular—one is tempted to say normal—feature of the economic system. Only free banking would have rendered the market economy secure against crises and depressions.[25]

The overwhelming source of the cyclical macroeconomic difficulties of recent years has clearly been the money supply shocks emanating from monetary authorities presiding over national fiat money regimes. A major threat to long-term planning is the fact that the purchasing power of money has become impossible to predict with any accuracy more than a few quarters into the future, because the nominal quantity of money is anchored to nothing more than the discretion of a monetary bureaucracy. In this environment the gold standard, which Keynes once derided as a "barbarous relic," has attracted new attention as a device for limiting the discretion of central banks. There is no question that a commitment to a fixed gold definition of the dollar would anchor the nominal quantity of money, make its purchasing power more predictable, and thereby promote coordination of long-term plans. But as far as damming the source of cyclical monetary disturbances, the gold standard is inadequate without free banking. A central bank tied to gold at a fixed parity can no longer inflate without limit in the long run, but it *can* manipulate in the short run the quantity of high-powered money, and thereby can subject the economy to monetary disruption—to what Mises calls "credit expansion with all its inevitable consequences."

A central bank that has the power to cause monetary disturbances inevitably will cause them. Central bankers, like central economic planners in general, typically lack the incentives and inevitably lack the information that would be necessary for them to perform as skillfully as a market system in matching supplies with demands. The incentive structure surrounding the monetary authorities is important because inflation and recession may often be the by-product of intentional policy actions. The public choice approach to government agencies suggests that government policymakers who are entrusted with control over money should be expected to succumb to the temptations of easy money.[26] The information problems of the monetary authorities are at least as important as these incentive problems. Even a "virtuous" central bank on a gold standard must make money supply errors because it lacks any timely and reliable signal of excess supply or demand for its liabilities. It is limited to such macroeconomic indicators as price indexes, interest rates, exchange rate movements within the gold points, and international gold flows. The information they give is either ambiguous or obvious only after an excess has already had its discoordinating effects, for example after an external drain has begun.[27]

Is Gold Necessary to Free Banking?

Quite conceivably free banking could be established in an economy with an outside money other than gold. Silver is an obvious alternative candidate. Supposing that bank liabilities are claims redeemable for silver coin rather than gold coin alters none of the analytical properties of a free banking system. If we take "free banking" to indicate a monetary system free not only from government regulation of the issue of inside money but also from government control over outside money, the field of potential outside monies is circumscribed only by the exclusion of actively issued government fiat money. Several sorts of nonfiat currencies beside gold and silver have had advocates in the past or present. A third candidate for potential free market outside money is "symmetalic" currency (or the vermeil standard, if you will), where the monetary unit is defined as so many grams of gold plus so many grams of silver. A fourth is currency redeemable for some nonmetallic (and nonmonetary) commodity or basket of commodities. A fifth is redeemable currency whose redemption rate is indexed to provide for stable purchasing power of the monetary unit. A sixth is inconvertible but privately issued currency.[28] Two further theoretical possibilities for elimination of government control over the quantity of outside currency also present themselves. The first of these is to freeze the stock of fiat money or the monetary base. The second is to have a payments system that makes no use of outside money.[29]

From a microsovereignty perspective all these sorts of currencies (with the exception of gold and silver) ought to be regarded as untried entrepreneurial ideas. The way to cut through the confusing welter of proposals in order to discover which one(s) money users would actually prefer to use is to let potential suppliers of the various currencies compete. This would require lifing any prohibitions, taxes, regulations, and legislated accounting rules that could serve as barriers to entry of alternative outside monies. The belief that none of the alternatives would lead to voluntary abandonment of an established precious metallic standard seems warranted by historical experience. But the question, given a microsovereignty ethic, ought not to be foreclosed by anticompetitive policies.

The burden of outcompeting an established standard is significant. Money users in an economy tend to converge on a single monetary standard for the reason, central to the emergence of money in the first place, that each trader finds it most convenient to use as a medium of exchange the item or items most readily accepted by other traders.[30] It is therefore difficult to convince any individual in a monetized economy to accept as a medium of exchange an asset that is neither a claim to something nor itself something that other individuals already accept as readily as money. In pondering the transition to open competition among monetary standards there is of course no a priori reason to consider gold or silver, rather than government fiat paper, vermeil, or plywood, as the proper initial monetary standard. The reason must instead be historical: It is gold and silver that emerged historically as money in advanced nations out of an invisible-hand convergence process driven by individual preferences. Gold and silver were chosen as money before governments got into the act of restricting monetary options. They voluntarily displaced other standards, presumably by more or less gradual diffusion and because they represented superior monies in the eyes of money users, in areas that came into trading contact with specie-using areas.[31]

While gold or silver is not logically necessary to free banking, then, respect for historically demonstrated consumer preferences suggests that a specie standard is the natural place to start.

Notes

1. Gerald P. O'Driscoll, Jr., "A Free-Market Money: Comment on Yeager," *Cato Journal* 3 (Spring 1983):327.

2. This example is taken from Allan H. Meltzer, "Monetary Reform in an Uncertain Environment," *Cato Journal* 3 (Spring 1983):97–105. Other examples of preferences attributed (without evidence) to consumers by monetary reformers would be preferences for higher real gross national product, more stable purchasing power of the monetary unit, and uniformity of money across producers.

3. In fact the relative instability and unpredictability of silver's purchasing power may have contributed to its abandonment in favor of gold during the nineteenth century. One would like to have a thorough interpretation of the historical evidence on this question, as governments' interests rather than individuals' preferences may have been responsible for switches from silver to gold.

4. The "compensated dollar" was the brainchild of Irving Fisher, who revived the quantity theory of money early in this century. See Irving Fisher, *Stabilizing the Dollar* (New York: Macmillan, 1920).

5. Phillip Cagan, "A Review of the Report of the Gold Commission and Some Thoughts on Convertible Monetary Systems," unpublished paper, Columbia University, October 1982, p. 4.

6. To use the terminology of Murray N. Rothbard, *Power and Market* (Menlo Park, Calif.: Institute for Humane Studies, 1970), complete individual sovereignty in the market requires the absence of triangular intervention. See also Donald C. Lavoie, "The Development of the Misesian Theory of Interventionism" in Israel M. Kirzner, ed., *Method, Process, and Austrian Economics* (Lexington, Mass.: Lexington Books, 1982), pp. 178–79 where Lavoie points out that certain forms of taxes constitute triangular intervention.

7. It should perhaps be noted explicitly that the so-called free banking systems in several American states between 1837 and 1863 did not meet these conditions. For a recent account of New York State's free banking experience see Robert G. King, "On the Economics of Private Money," *Journal of Monetary Economics* 12 (July 1983):139–56.

8. For American experience with private mints in the Appalachian and Californian gold-producing regions, see Donald H. Kagin, *Private Gold Coins and Patterns of the United States* (New York: Arco, 1981). For an early free trade defense of exclusively private coinage, see Thomas Hodgskin, *Popular Political Economy* (London: Charles Tait, 1827; reprint ed., New York: Augustus M. Kelley, 1966), pp. 190–96. For a recent defense see Rothbard, *Power and Market*, pp. 59–60, where Rothbard points out that only competitive private coinage can be presumed to give consumers the denominations of coins they want.

9. For an evolutionary perspective on monetary institutions, see Lawrence H. White, "Competitive Payments Systems and the Unit of Account," *American Economic Review 74* (September 1984):699–712. On the early history of European banking see Raymond de Roover, *Business, Banking, and Economic Thought in Late Medieval and Early Modern Europe* (Chicago: University of Chicago Press, 1956), ch. 5. See also Ludwig von Mises, *The Theory of Money and Credit*, new enlarged ed. (Irvington-on-Hudson, N.Y.: Foundation for Economic Education, 1971), pp. 278–80.

10. See Mises, *Theory of Money and Credit*, pp. 50–53.

11. King, "On the Economics of Private Money," p. 154, affirms this conclusion for New York State's experience, Lawrence H. White, *Free Banking in Britain* (Cambridge, England: Cambridge University Press, 1984), p. 146, affirms it for Scotland's experience with free banking.

12. See White, *Free Banking in Britain*, pp. 7–8.

13. Lawrence H. White, "Competitive Money, Inside and Out," *Cato Journal 3* (Spring 1983):292. I am grateful to David Price for bringing this question to my attention.

14. See Milton Friedman and Anna Jacobson Schwartz, *A Monetary History of the United States, 1867–1960* (Princeton, N.J.: Princeton University Press, 1963), p. 56n.

15. Ludwig von Mises, *Human Action*, 3rd ed. (Chicago: Henry Regnery, 1966), pp. 445–47.

16. Murray N. Rothbard, *The Mystery of Banking* (New York: Richardson and Snyder, 1983), pp. 97, 100.

17. Ibid., pp. 93–94, briefly relates the legal precedents on this question.

18. Specimens of Scottish banknotes may be found in S.G. Checkland, *Scottish Banking: A History, 1695–1973* (Glasgow: Collins, 1975), pp. 32, 67, 98, 105, 185, 383, 546–48.

19. On the title-transfer model, see Williamson M. Evers, "Toward Reformulation of the Law of Contracts," *Journal of Libertarian Studies 1* (Winter 1977): 3–13. I would argue that the title-transfer view is uniquely compatible with an ethic of individual sovereignty.

20. On the option clause in early Scotland, see Checkland, *Scottish Banking*, pp. 67–68, 82, 110. The law banning them in 1765 met with Adam Smith's approval: see *The Wealth of Nations*, edited by R.H. Campbell and A.S. Skinner (Indianapolis: Liberty Classics, 1981), pp. 325–26, 329. It should be noted that the option clauses in Scottish banknotes specified an interest yield (5 percent per annum) in case of deferred redemption, and specified the period of deferral (six months). A representative "optional" note read: "The Royal Bank of Scotland... is hereby obliged to pay to _____ or the Bearer, one pound sterling on demand, or, in the Option of the Directors, one pound six pence sterling at the End of Six Months after the day of the demand...". Checkland, *Scottish Banking*, p. 67, provides a specimen. This interest penalty, imposed by competition, further discouraged banks from exercising the option.

21. Comprehensive referencing of this literature would take a long article by itself. On the early nineteenth-century literature, see White, *Free Banking in Britain*, chs. 3,4. Classic works in the Austrian monetary theory of the business

cycle include Ludwig von Mises, *On the Manipulation of Money and Credit* (Dobbs Ferry, N.Y.: Free Market Books, 1978) and F.A. Hayek, *Prices and Production*, 2nd ed. (New York: Augustus M. Kelley, 1967). Important works in the Monetarist tradition include Friedman and Schwartz, *A Monetary History of the United States, 1867–1960*, and Robert E. Lucas, Jr., *Studies in Business Cycle Theory* (Cambridge, Mass.: MIT Press, 1981).

22. This and the following paragraph draw upon White, *Free Banking in Britain*, pp. 14–19.

23. Again see White, *Free Banking in Britain*, ch. 3 and ch. 4, sec. 3.

24. For an example of fairly sophisticated argument along these lines by a leading Jacksonian theoretician see William Leggett, "Bank of the United States" in *Democratick Editorials*, edited by Lawrence H. White (Indianapolis: Liberty Press, 1984).

25. Ludwig von Mises, *Human Action*, p. 443.

26. Mises, ibid., quite bluntly blamed actual central bank overexpansions either on deliberate attempts to cheapen credit by politicians catering to popular inflationist ideology or on attempts at inflationary finance. For a valuable survey article explaining both the incentive and information problems of central banking, see Pamela Brown, "Constitution or Competition? Alternative Approaches to Monetary Reform," *Literature of Liberty* 5 (Autumn 1982):7–52.

27. On this point see the remarkably perceptive statements of Samuel Bailey, *A Defence of Joint-Stock Banks and Country Issues* (London: James Ridgway, 1840). Several pertinent passages from this work are quoted in White, *Free Banking in Britain*, pp. 130–33.

28. I have given a similar list, and further discussed the question addressed by this section, in "Gold, Dollars, and Private Currencies," *Policy Report* 3 (June 1981):6–11. Some combination of the fourth and fifth sorts of nonfiat currency has recently been suggested by Robert E. Hall, "Explorations in the Gold Standard and Related Policies for Stabilizing the Dollar," in Hall, ed., *Inflation: Causes and Effects* (Chicago: University of Chicago Press, 1982), pp. 111–22. Hall proposes a basket standard composed of ammonium nitrate, copper, aluminum, and plywood.

29. A base freeze is proposed by R.H. Timberlake, Jr., "Monetization Practices and the Political Structure of the Federal Reserve System," Cato Institute *Policy Analysis* (August 12, 1981):12. The idea of a cashless competitive payments system is explored by Robert L. Greenfield and Leland B. Yeager, "A Laissez-Faire Approach to Monetary Stability," *Journal of Money, Credit, and Banking* 15 (August 1983):302–15, and proposed as a reform by Leland B. Yeager, "Stable Money and Free-Market Currencies," *Cato Journal* 3 (Spring 1983):323–25. I criticize on evolutionary grounds the idea that competition would give rise to a cashless payments system, or to a basket standard, in "Competitive Payments System and the Unit of Account."

30. The *locus classicus* for this theory of the origin of money is Carl Menger, "On the Origin of Money," *Economic Journal* 2 (1892):239–55.

31. Sweden, for example, had a copper standard in early times. The relative cumbersomeness of this should be obvious.

7

The Political and Economic Agenda for a Real Gold Standard

Ron Paul

O ne of the basic insights of the great Austrian economists, both Carl Menger and Ludwig von Mises, is that money emerged by evolution from the market process. It was not invented by governments. There are basic economic forces today that are contributing to the further evolution of the monetary system, and there is a political strategy that I believe will make it possible to liberate those forces and restore the monetary role for gold. Because of the current economic and political climate, it is important to understand what we can do—and what we cannot hope to do in the short run.

The Political Climate for Reform

In his 1952 epilogue to *The Theory of Money and Credit,* Mises included a section with the title, "The United States' Return to a Sound Currency."[1] The Korean War inflation was fresh in most people's minds that year, when Mises prepared his proposal. Food prices in 1951 had jumped 11.1 percent, with consumer prices in general jumping 7.9 percent. Yet by the mid-1950s, the public interest in monetary reform seemed to abate. Changes in the consumer price index were in the vicinity of 1 percent per year for the next decade, and food prices even declined in 1952–53.

The political and economic agenda for creating a real gold standard in the United States—a new international gold standard led by monetary reform in this country—depends very much upon the climate of political and economic opinion. If the Korean War inflation had continued, I believe Ludwig von Mises' proposal would have received much wider attention.

For help in the preparation of this chapter, I would like to acknowledge with gratitude the research of Joe Cobb, professional staff member of the Committee on Banking, Finance, and Urban Affairs of the U.S. House of Representatives.

My belief that periods of monetary disorder always focus attention on gold as the solution is strengthened by the recent occasion of a congressionally mandated Gold Commission, on which I was proud to serve. It was created in response to the high rates of inflation in the late 1970s and a rising cry from the general public to restore gold to its rightful monetary role.

Most people know of the Gold Commission merely what the press reported—that it rejected a return to the gold standard. I believe the true significance of the Gold Commission is that the politicians and central bankers were so alarmed at such a thing that they made sure it was packed by an array of Keynesians and monetarists. These advocates of the established institutions and arrangements certainly don't want any role for gold to threaten their cozy theories about scientific monetary management and macroeconomic planning.

The dramatic reduction in average price increases during the recent recession has once again diverted attention from fundamental monetary reform, but it is clear to me that our present unstable arrangement will break down once more, and there will be another Gold Commission in the future.

The Mises Proposal

I want briefly to review the plan Mises described, and then set down the steps I believe would achieve his goal. Any differences in the proposals I am supporting in Congress from the plan he described in 1952 are based on my judgments about the progressive deterioration in our monetary and fiscal system during the intervening thirty years and the politics of the task today.

In *The Theory of Money and Credit*, Mises wrote: "The first step must be a radical and unconditional abandonment of any further inflation."[2] Although I strongly support this objective, I do not believe it would ever be possible to achieve such a requirement if we place it as "the first step."

Banishing inflation is, in fact, the ultimate objective we expect to achieve by creating a new gold standard. The U.S. government has moved so far in the direction of fiscal irresponsibility that the reform of our basic monetary and financial institutions has become much more complex. For political reasons, ending inflation cannot be the "first" step. We must subdivide it into many smaller preparatory steps even to approach the task.

Happily, the second step that Mises described has already been achieved: "All restrictions on trading and holding gold must be repealed."[3]

In January 1975 it became legal for Americans to own and trade gold, and in 1977 the remaining prohibitions on gold clauses in contracts were repealed. In my view, this restoration of liberty is the most important change in circumstances since 1952, and the one condition that is today most favorable to the restoration of gold to its proper monetary role.

One of the points on which Mises was adamant is the role of the Federal Reserve System: "It is essential for the reform suggested that the Federal Reserve System should be kept out of its way."[4] Mises advocated the creation of a "Conversion Agency" that would be responsible for issuing gold coins and bullion to the public, and redeeming excess quantities of gold in circulation if the public should choose to exchange gold for paper. The Federal Reserve would continue to have some responsibility under his plan, as a fiscal agent for the Treasury in managing the national debt, but the Conversion Agency would maintain the domestic and international exchange value of the dollar.

This is one of the most distinctive differences between Mises and other advocates of the gold standard, who want the Federal Reserve to buy and sell gold at a fixed conversion for dollars. The government's fiscal agent necessarily performs a banking function as it collects and disburses tax money. It would have to be separate from a conversion agency that would function more like an office of the National Bureau of Standards than like a bank. Mises' analysis of financial institutions and the market process led him to favor free, decentralized banking.[5] He was thus a consistent advocate of a separation of powers.

Ludwig von Mises understood that the problem with monetary institutions is first of all a political problem. By proposing this separation of powers between the central bank and a conversion agency, he was an early proponent of an institutionalized competition in currency. Even the government of a constitutional republic like the United States could not be trusted with discretionary monetary power: "The President, Congress, and the Supreme Court have clearly proved their inability or unwillingness to protect the common man, the voter, from being victimized by inflationary machinations. The function of securing a sound currency must pass into new hands, into those of the whole nation."[6] Restoring the monetary role for gold must become a popular crusade in the United States. In the political sphere, popular crusades require tangible—as opposed to ideological or intellectual—benefits that people can recognize and subscribe to.

The First Step—Gold Coinage

The heart of Mises' proposal to restore gold to our monetary system is a gold coinage. He wrote: "Gold must be in the cash holdings of everyone.

Everybody must see gold coins changing hands, must be used to having gold coins in his pockets, to receiving gold coins when he cashes his paycheck, and to spending gold coins when he buys in a store."[7] In this one detail—the critical importance of the gold coinage—I believe lies the key to establishing a new gold standard.

We should make no mistake about it: The more progress we make toward reestablishing the gold standard, the more aggressive our opposition will become. Some vested interests, as you know, have a lot to lose if we succeed in getting the monetary system reconstructed on a gold basis. The first political step is, therefore, to get the coinage into circulation.

One objective might be to aim for every American to become a gold owner. We must encourage a broader base of political support for gold ownership and the availability of gold for personal economic objectives. Certainly a broader base of gold ownership in the country would help to reduce the threats of discriminatory taxation or regulation of gold ownership and gold coin transactions, which are seriously favored in Congress today.

Ludwig von Mises and most advocates of a gold coin standard have understood the coinage as something similar to what we had in the nineteenth century, until 1933. Under this concept, coins would be various sizes, with face values in "dollars" but not exact sizes in any system of weights. We could advocate a coinage of $50.00 denominations, about one-eleventh of an ounce, or $100.00 denominations, about one-fifth ounce; but that would start the process of rebuilding the gold monetary system at the wrong end. It would require, first, a majority in Congress to vote to establish a new par value for the dollar.

By starting with the necessity for a congressional majority to decide on the sizes and weights of gold coins, we must presume in advance that we know the "correct" par value for the dollar. We must presume that a majority of the public already supports the restoration of a gold standard. The political task becomes a gigantic educational problem. Before anything constructive could be accomplished, millions of people who understand nothing about the causes of inflation or the advantage of a free market monetary system would have to be persuaded to join a political movement. All the misconceptions that are propounded today by academic economists, all the mysticism of the central bankers, all the objections of the politicians would have to be expunged from the popular mind. I do not believe this would be an efficient way to approach the problem.

What we must first do is get the coinage into circulation, and then build the political base to lock the government's fiscal folly with golden handcuffs. People have always understood the tangible value of gold coins in circulation. They don't need to agree or even understand the fine points of monetary theory to own gold coins, trade gold coins, or use gold coins to satisfy part of their marginal utility demand for cash balances.

Most people understand very little about economics or monetary theory. When they see supposed experts in disagreement, the status quo wins by default, because nobody with the power to change it has the courage of conviction. The majority of voters see the debate among experts and hesitate to support any leaders with comprehensive reform schemes. This is why all efforts to rebuild a gold monetary system have met with frustration and stalemate in the past.

The demonstrated popularity in the United States of Krugerrand coins, and all the imitators of the Krugerrand (Maple Leaf, Panda, Onza, and the U.S. Gold medallions) have shown us that it is possible to adopt another tactic, that of getting gold coins into circulation prior to setting a new par value for the dollar. Indeed, the only affirmative recommendation of the Gold Commission was to create a new U.S. gold coinage in units of weight.

I would love to see a purely private, free market monetary system with any honest manufacturer able to produce coins, as Americans saw in California from 1849 to 1864. There must certainly be no restrictions on the private production of coins, but I believe that getting the U.S. Mint further into the act, producing a gold coinage with some of the mystique of the government, will be useful in the further political stages of monetary reform. Honest money, after all, is a political objective; it is fitting that people should demand honesty from their government, as well as an economic policy that permits individuals to compete honestly. An official coinage that reflects honest bullion weights is a powerful symbol of the gold standard we support.

The Transition to a Gold Standard

The coinage should be based on exact units of bullion weight. The coins should be denominated in troy ounces, half-ounces, and smaller sizes if feasible. The denomination of the coinage is the secret to our success in the later stages of the political agenda, so let me take a few moments to explain the central importance of the denominations.

There are several important advantages to starting with a gold coinage denominated in troy ounce and fractional units of an ounce. Since the unit of money should be defined as a definite weight of bullion, a coinage denominated by units of troy weight contributes significantly to the reeducation of the public. This knowledge, which is now almost completely lost to three generations of Americans, must be reimplanted.

Murray N. Rothbard has made this point most forcefully:

> The transition from gold to fiat money will be greatly smoothed if the State has previously abandoned ounces, grams, grains, and other units of weight in naming its monetary units and substituted unique names, such as dollar, mark, franc, etc. It will then be far easier to eliminate the public's association of monetary units with weight and to teach the public to value the names themselves. Furthermore, if each national government sponsors its own unique name, it will be far easier for each State to control its own fiat issue absolutely.[8]

Some writers have resisted the suggestion of a coinage denominated only by units of weight, arguing that the "dollar" was originally a unit of weight; but I think this is a misstatement. "Dollar" was the name of a coin that had a definite weight, but it was not a "unit" of weight. Adopting the name of the standard unit of bullion weight as the denomination of the coinage will bring together two important concepts about money that we must actively teach to a majority of Americans if we are ever going to restore a gold standard. The educational job becomes that much easier.

Second, as Mises understood, the Federal Reserve and existing banks have to be kept separate from the remonetization of gold until the progress of popular support is broad and deep enough that special interest lobbying will not pervert the system. By avoiding any use of a dollar denomination on the coins, the Federal Reserve System is automatically kept out of the picture during this developmental period. The dollar denomination is today a monopoly trademark for the Federal Reserve System.

Third, when the date finally arrives, at the end of the transition period, to provide the U.S. dollar with a fixed definition in terms of gold, it will be a very easy detail to announce to the public that the conversion agency stipulated by Mises is starting to buy and resell the troy ounce coins at a fixed price. The dollar was defined as 25.8 grains of standard gold in 1900. Today it might be defined as one grain of standard 0.900 gold. There is nothing inconsistent with this requirement if the coins are denominated in troy ounce, half-ounce, or quarter-ounce sizes.

In Mises' monetary reform proposal, and under the classical gold standard, the various substitutes for coin—bank notes, bank drafts and acceptances, and demand deposits—are supposed to be fixed in value to the underlying coin and exchangeable for it. The conversion agency would function as a resale buyer and wholesale distributor of the coins, and equally as a buyer of last resort for the paper money of the Federal Reserve.

The question that is most difficult to answer about the transition to a new gold standard is how long it should take. The transition plan envisioned by Mises called for a period of time in which the free market in gold discovered the new parity rate that would produce neither inflation nor deflation. "It is probable that the price of gold established after some oscillations on the American market will be higher than $35 per ounce... maybe somewhere between $36 and $38, perhaps even somewhat higher. Once the market price has attained some stability, the time has come to decree this market rate as the new legal parity of the dollar and to secure its unconditional convertibility at this parity."[9] Mises did not discuss how long this transition period should last before fixing the new par value for the dollar, but it would have to last as long as it might take to build a political majority. This is almost a truism, because Congress would have to enact legislation to fix the gold weight of the U.S. dollar.

The choice for advocates of a gold coin monetary system, therefore, is straightforward: either we move ahead with a program for U.S. gold coins denominated by weight, with no face value in terms of dollars—thereby starting the transition period immediately—or we sit on our hands, perhaps for decades, debating the fine points of banking theory, until the paper money system collapses around us. Even then, it is not obvious that the collapse of the paper money system would bring about the political pressure necessary to restore a gold standard. We might end up with controls on wages, prices, credit, and exchange controls instead of a gold coin standard.

Longer-Term Benefits of Bullion-Weight Coinage

Over the longer term, assuming the transition to a new gold standard is successful (with Congress enacting a gold value for the dollar and fiscal policy disciplined by monetary convertibility), there are still distinct advantages to retaining the coinage in units of troy weight rather than assigning an official, stamped dollar value on the face of the coins.

First, Gresham's law—Bad money drives out good—tends to affect even the most perfect gold coin standard. If we want gold coins to circulate freely in an economy where all prices are quoted in dollars, the coins themselves should not be denominated in dollars. Gresham's law operates even when bank notes are 100 percent warehouse receipts for gold. People might be able to trust that bank notes are fully backed by gold, but given the choice of which to spend and which to keep in the cash box, the paper will be spent and the coin will be saved because each monetary instrument has its own subjective value qualities.

The mere fact that honest coins are more secure than even the most secure paper is a sufficient qualitative difference to give them a premium

value. The subjective evaluation of every person in the free market economy must be employed to help keep the monetary system honest and
noninflationary. To assure that gold coins move in active commerce,
rather than sitting in vaults, we must let free market pricing operate. Let
the coins command a slight premium everywhere except at the conversion agency, which would have to redeem any excess Federal Reserve
dollar bank notes (token money) for honest coin at the par value in
response to public demand.

Gresham's law is a natural consequence of price fixing, mandating
the exchange of items with different marginal utilities at a ratio not
determined by the free market. It is, in fact, a special case of setting a
price by law slightly too low for gold coins, the preferred form of money
for long-term savings. Only the conversion agency should be mandated
by law to exchange genuine coin for paper dollars at the par value. There
are costs in terms of real resources, opportunity costs in the operations of
a gold coin monetary system. These costs are worth paying; they must be
paid to have an operational monetary constitution that prevents financial exploitation, but the issue of "Who pays?" must also be considered.

Most economists who support a gold coin standard do not recognize
the importance of distributing the marginal costs of coinage throughout
the entire spectrum of the monetary economy. In the nineteenth century,
this system of fixing the face value of gold coins in terms of paper bank
notes, rather than by units of weight, led to the centralization of gold
hoards in bank vaults, which made it all the easier for governments to
confiscate them. The simple confusion of the coin and the denomination
of the money produced the effect of Gresham's law during the classical
period. If it is left up to the government, the central bank, or the banking
system to absorb the costs of having coin always on hand to redeem bank
notes at face value, the managers at each stage will attempt to economize
these costs, rather than charging the consumer for them, and there will
be a constant pressure to take coins out of circulation and replace them
with substitutes: paper bank notes and demand deposits.

If the coinage is denominated only in terms of troy ounces and fractions of an ounce, the free market pricing structure takes care of this
problem instantly and effortlessly. The official conversion agency must
redeem Federal Reserve notes at par, but others should be free to charge a
competitive premium for gold coins (that is, to discount Federal Reserve
notes). This would tend to assure a continuing flow of gold coins into
private ownership.

Ludwig von Mises proposed to solve this problem by forcing the
circulation of gold coins by prohibiting any paper bank notes in the $5,
$10, and $20 denominations. In 1952 it seemed reasonable to him that
the dollar might be worth something nearer 1/40th ounce, so gold coins

could replace those denominations. Today only the $100 bill would be affected by this proposal, since gold coins now would be too tiny for most commercial transactions. Where they would find most popular utility would be in financial transactions and in the purchase of consumer durables, because of the generally higher prices. Over time, the Federal Reserve dollar will come to be recognized as a form of token money that is just a tiny fraction of a gold ounce.

We can only make political use of the fact that the public treasures hard money over paper money if we make it clear that there is a difference. A different denomination for each form—"dollars" for paper and "troy ounces" for coin—is the easiest and most obvious way to achieve this objective. There is a specious similarity in this proposal to the gold exchange standard of the 1920s, but the active circulation of small denomination gold coins would defeat any such criticism. The denial of any small denomination coins was the distinguishing feature of the pseudo gold standard adopted in the 1920s and perpetuated under the Bretton Woods arrangement in 1944.

So long as the conversion agency performed its role, it would also be impossible for the Federal Reserve System to produce a monetary inflation because the conversion agency, which would be completely separate from the government's banking activities, would be engaged in the process of absorbing excess dollars from circulation, in exchange for troy ounce coins that it issues. If the Federal Reserve made the opposite mistake, as it has often done in the past, of overly restricting the money supply, the market could always sell coins to the conversion agency to obtain any dollars demanded. A precise balance would be achieved between the general public's demand for money in the form of coin and its demand in the form of bank notes or deposit account with banks by the existence of the conversion agency as something separate from the Federal Reserve.

Agenda for Monetary Reform

The genius of Ludwig von Mises was his profound insight into the free market process, the science of catallactics. The most important thing I have learned from his work is that the achievement of a new gold standard in our society will have to come from the free market itself. This is why I believe the first step must be a new troy ounce gold coinage, even without any legal tender qualities or special tax treatment. As we have found in recent banking deregulation, the market develops new procedures and techniques in the monetary and financial system, and Congress follows with repeal of old, restrictive laws. This is the political and economic dynamic process that we also can harness to restore gold to its proper monetary role.

All the government needs to do is to get out of the way. The political and economic agenda for monetary reform, therefore, consists of the following steps:

1. Congress must adopt the legislation recommended by the Gold Commission to bring a new U.S. gold coinage into circulation, denominated only in troy ounce units and fractions thereof.
2. Advocates of the remonetization of gold must work both in the political arena and in the marketplace to get as many of these new coins into the possession of the public as possible. Politically, this means resisting taxation or any regulations on the utility of the new gold coins for purposes of exchange either for other goods and services or for dollars. As Ludwig von Mises demonstrated in his *Theory of Money and Credit*,[10] it is the marketability of a good that gives it a monetary character. The more easily recognized and marketable the new gold coinage becomes, the more it will be recognized as genuine pieces of money.
3. The fact that the troy ounce of gold is well defined and the paper dollar has no fixed referent at all should be made the focus of continued education and debate, just as we are now doing. The continuing academic work by students of Carl Menger and Ludwig von Mises in monetary and financial theory is vitally important, particularly to expose the fallacies of centralized macroeconomic planning and the failure of "managed money." The acquiescence of the economics profession, which is today disdainful of gold, will have to be secured. Serious academic work will stimulate interest in a new Gold Commission, which would be able to focus this research in economic theory on the political issue of monetary reform. It is essential to move the center of monetary debate from the question of how the central bank should perform monetary management to the more general question of managed money versus market-process money.
4. The objective would remain to persuade a majority of Congress to enact a new par value for the U.S. dollar in terms of gold. When every American family is familiar with gold coins and understands the intrinsic defects in a managed paper standard, a majority in Congress can be persuaded by the demands of voters to enact a new par value for the U.S. dollar and to establish the conversion agency described by Mises.

Except for random shocks in the financial markets, due to Federal Reserve central planning mistakes, and occasional political disturbances, such as a Middle East war or troubles in South Africa, the dollar value of the troy ounce coins should stabilize, just as we saw in 1984. The old myth that "gold is too unstable to serve as money" will be disproven by the common popular experience.

The strategy set forth in these four steps, I believe, is the only politically feasible way it can be done. All of the wishful thinking about restoring the gold standard by electing the "right person" to be president, or by attempting to educate the general public, will fail without first making available a tangible gold coinage as something they can see, touch, use for a portion of their savings, and become accustomed to using for many kinds of transactions. Public opinion polls have shown strong support for monetary stability. There is substantial support for a gold standard among the American public, yet the various proposals for enacting a par value for the dollar are dismissed by congressmen, the financial and business press, and "experts" of all stripes.

The task at hand, therefore, is to remove every roadblock to the realization of the will of the majority. The sentiment for gold must be mobilized. The question is no longer "Why do we need a gold standard?" but "How do we get it enacted?" To restore the gold standard to its central role in our system of constitutional government, we must lead a second kind of American revolution, a popular movement for honest money. As Mises wrote: "Without such a check all other constitutional safeguards can be rendered vain."[11] The gold standard as a constitutional restraint on our government was abolished in the United States, not in 1934 nor in 1971, but in 1819 with the U.S. Supreme Court case of *McCulloch v. Maryland*.[12] With this famous Supreme Court interpretation of the Constitution, the federal government acquired the sovereign power to manipulate the nation's money, from which the legal tender laws of the Civil War, the central banking powers of the Federal Reserve System, and the ultimate prohibition on any private use of gold as money in 1934 derived. This link between sovereignty and currency manipulation has been ably argued by Henry Mark Holzer.[13]

The key to the government's power to manipulate money is its control over the definition of the word "dollar." A troy ounce coinage in widespread circulation would significantly alter the public's perception of the government's monetary role. If the Congress should ever attempt to change the par value of the dollar in terms of the gold coinage, the holders of coins would be fully protected. Financial promises to pay coins would be protected, in a way that promises to pay dollars would not be. Best of all, as a result of the separation of currency and coin denominations, there would be no public purpose served by asking citizens to turn in old coins for new ones; the crime of January 1934 would not be repeated.

Restoring a gold coinage is also the highest duty we now face, as citizens of this country. We no longer live in a world where the free market is taken for granted. On the contrary, most people assume government must control and guide the economic system for the benefit of all. Ludwig von Mises suffered during most of his career because he understood too well the stakes of this ideological conflict:

> "Cynics dispose of the advocacy of the restitution of the gold standard by calling it utopian. Yet we have only the choice between two utopias: the utopia of a market economy, not paralysed by government sabotage, on the one hand, and the utopia of totalitarian all-round planning on the other hand. The choice of the first alternative implies the decision in favour of the gold standard."[14]

I believe the goal of a market economy, not paralyzed by government sabotage on behalf of vested interests and pressure groups is an ideal worth fighting for. This is why I first ran for Congress, and it is the only reason I believe justifies political action.

Notes

1. Ludwig von Mises [1952], *The Theory of Money and Credit* (Irvington-on-Hudson, New York: Foundation for Economic Education, 1971), pp. 448–52.
2. Ibid., p. 448.
3. Ibid.
4. Ibid., p. 450.
5. Ibid., pp. 395–99.
6. Ibid., p. 452.
7. Ibid., pp. 450–51.
8. Murray N. Rothbard, *Man, Economy and State* (Los Angeles: Nash, 1970), p. 941n.
9. Mises, *Theory of Money and Credit*, p. 449.
10. Ibid., pp. 30–34.
11. Ibid., p. 452.
12. 17 U.S. 316.
13. Henry Mark Holzer, *Government's Money Monopoly* (New York: Books in Focus, 1981).
14. Mises, *Theory of Money and Credit*, p. 457.

Index

Monetary Stabilization and Cyclical
  Policy (Mises), 37
Monetary standard, Heilperin's definition of, 102
Money: commodity, costs of, 66–67;
  confusion between capital and,
  44–45; demand for, xv, 21–22, 36,
  64, 65–66; "denationalization" of,
  2–5, 57n; history of, 43–45;
  Menger's theory of origin of, xiii,
  xiv–xv, 19, 20–21; nonneutrality
  of, 37–43, 44, 48, 73; objective
  exchange value of, 25; as organic
  outgrowth of market economy,
  106; purchasing power of, 23–25,
  58n–59n, 123–24; "rarity value" of,
  24–25; resource costs and, 70–71;
  role as unit of value, 74; sound, 48,
  49, 74; subjective value theory of,
  19, 22, 23, 25; velocity of circulation of, 36, 53n–54n
"Money and Coinage since 1857"
  (Menger), 31
Money market, 44
Money supply: errors, 121–24;
  government monopoly over, 1–3,
  57n
Morgenstern, Oskar, 35
Multicurrency circulation, 5
Mundell, Robert, 102

National Bank Act of 1863, 119
National demand for money, 22
National price level concept, 90–91
Natural rate of interest, 40–41,
  52n–53n, 54n
Nature and Significance of Economic
  Science, The (Robbins), 35
Nelson, R.W., 40
Neutral money policy, 40–43, 46–48,
  78n
"Nirvana approach," 78n
Nixon, Richard, 10, 90
Nonneutrality of money, 37–43, 44,
  48

O'Driscoll, Gerald P., Jr., xiv, 111
One hundred percent gold reserve,
  13–14, 49, 120
One hundred percent gold standard,
  110n

"On Our Currency" (Menger), 20, 25
Open-market operations, 32, 85–86
Opportunity costs, x, 67, 77n, 136
Option clauses in bank notes, 127n
Ownership of gold, 132–34, 136

Palyi, Melchior, xii, 104, 105–6
Paper standard. See Fiat money
Parity rate, 51, 94–95, 135
Paterson, Isabel, 15n–16n
Paul, Ron, 13
Peacetime, monetary expansion in, 1
Phillips, C.A., 40
Pigou, A.C., 72
Plato, definition of money by, 21
Poincaré reforms, 95
Political climate for reform, 129–30
Political feasibility of constant price
  level, 73–74
Popular movement, need for, 139
Positivist view, 63
Precious metals, preference for, 7–8
Price: -adjustment costs, 64–65,
  68–70; automatic equilibration of
  balance of payments and, 83–85;
  concept of, 9; cumulative rise or
  fall in, 36, 43; fixing, 9, 103–4, 136;
  rule, gold, x–xi, 106–7, 116
Price level: concept of, 6; constant, 6,
  65–67, 71–75; consumer, 71,
  99–100; inelasticity of gold supply
  and, 68–69; national, 90–91; stabilization, 41, 46–47, 86, 89, 115–16;
  stabilization, international gold
  standard and domestic, 90–101;
  types of, 69; welfare maximizing
  rate of change of, 72
Price-specie-flow mechanism, 84
Principles of Economics (Menger),
  19–20, 23
Private mints, 126n
Privatization of dollar, 2–5
Production: gold, 26–27, 51, 64, 65–66;
  nonneutrality of money and effect
  on, 37–39, 41–42; process, 36, 39
Pseudo gold standard, xii, 12
Purchasing power of money, 23–25,
  58n–59n, 123–24, 126n
"Purchasing Power of the Austrian
  Guilder, The" (Menger), 20,
  23–24

Wartime, expansion of money supply in, 1

Welfare-maximizing rate of change of price level, 72

Wicksell, Knut, 38, 43, 52n–53n

Wieser, Friedrich von, 25, 35, 36

World War I, effect on gold standard, 1, 48–49, 104–5

Editor and Contributors

Llewellyn H. Rockwell, Jr., is director of The Ludwig von Mises Institute at Auburn University.

Richard M. Ebeling is assistant professor of economics at the University of Dallas.

Roger W. Garrison is assistant professor of economics at Auburn University.

Ron Paul was a member of the U.S. House of Representatives and its Banking Committee from 1976–84.

Murray N. Rothbard is professor of economics at New York Polytechnic Institute.

Joseph T. Salerno is assistant professor of economics at Rutgers University.

Hans F. Sennholz is professor of economics at Grove City College.

Lawrence H. White is assistant professor of economics at New York University.

Leland B. Yeager is professor of economics at Auburn University.